THE CHILDREN OF LIGHT
AND
THE CHILDREN OF DARKNESS

BIOGRAPHICAL NOTE

After receiving his BD and MA degrees from Yale Divinity School in 1914 and 1915, respectively, Dr. Niebuhr served as a pastor in Detroit for thirteen years. In 1928 he joined the faculty of Union Theological Seminary, New York, as Professor of Christian Ethics and remained there until his retirement in 1960. Dr. Niebuhr held honorary degrees from Oxford, Glasgow University, Columbia, Harvard, Princeton, Yale, and a host of other colleges and universities in the United States and abroad. In 1939 he became the fifth American to be invited to deliver the famous Gifford Lectures at Edinburgh University. Dr. Niebuhr was a member of the Academy of Arts and Letters and in 1964 was given the Presidential Freedom Award for Distinguished Service. He died in 1971.

The Children of Light
and the
Children of Darkness

A VINDICATION OF DEMOCRACY

AND A CRITIQUE OF

ITS TRADITIONAL DEFENSE

REINHOLD NIEBUHR

With a new introduction by **GARY DORRIEN**

The University of Chicago Press
Chicago & London

The University of Chicago Press, Chicago 60637
Copyright © 1944 by Charles Scribner's Sons
Renewal copyright © 1972 by Ursula Keppel-Compton Niebuhr
Foreword to the 1960 edition copyright © 1960 by Reinhold Niebuhr
Introduction © 2011 by Gary Dorrien
All rights reserved.
University of Chicago Press edition 2011
Printed in the United States of America

20 19 18 17 16 15 14 13 12 11   1 2 3 4 5

ISBN-13: 978-0-226-58400-3 (paper)
ISBN-10: 0-226-58400-3 (paper)

Library of Congress Cataloging-in-Publication Data

Niebuhr, Reinhold, 1892–1971.
The children of light and the children of darkness : a vindication of democracy and a critique of its traditional defense / by Reinhold Niebuhr ; with a new introduction by Gary Dorrien.
    p. cm.
ISBN-13: 978-0-226-58400-3 (pbk. : alk. paper)
ISBN-10: 0-226-58400-3 (pbk. : alk. paper) 1. Democracy. I. Title.
JC423.N5 2011
321.8—DC22
                                        2011005928

♾ This paper meets the requirements of ANSI/NISO Z39.48-1992
(Permanence of Paper).

TO

My friend, colleague and chief,

HENRY SLOANE COFFIN

"The children of this world are in their generation wiser than the children of light."

Lk. 16:8.

CONTENTS

INTRODUCTION

REINHOLD NIEBUHR got to be the leading
American Christian social ethicist of the twentieth century partly by changing his politics in every
decade of his career. He began, in his twenties, as a
liberal advocate of U.S. intervention in World War I.
In the 1920s he became a pacifist and Social Gospel
idealist. In the 1930s he dropped pacifism and Social Gospel idealism, blasting the New Deal from a
militantly Socialist position. In the 1940s he left the
Socialist Party and subsequently dropped Socialism,
assuming a leadership role in a prointerventionist co-
alition of politicians, trade unionists, and intellectuals,
the Union for Democratic Action (UDA). In the late
1940s and early 1950s, as a pillar of the Democratic
Party's "Vital Center" establishment, he became a
chief apologist of the United States' Cold War against
Communism. In the late 1950s he began to protest
that the Cold War had been militarized and ideolo-
gized beyond anything necessary to U.S. national interest. In the early 1960s he supported America's intervention in Vietnam, but he 1966 he turned against

it, protesting that the war in Vietnam undermined U.S. interests and was morally indefensible. There were a few constants among all the changes. Niebuhr took for granted the activist orientation of the Social Gospel, even as he denounced Social Gospel idealism. He was deeply political, for which he never apologized; if people suffered because of politics and economics, Christian ethics had to deal with politics and economics. He was a brilliant interpreter of human fallibility, sin, and ambiguity. And he was always determined to be realistic, even during his Social Gospel pacifist phase, taking seriously that good and evil are inextricably linked in human nature and society.

The Children of Light and the Children of Darkness, written at midcareer as Niebuhr was coming fully into his own, is the most comprehensive statement of his political philosophy. Not coincidentally, Niebuhr was near the end of his Socialist phase when he wrote it. In November 1943, while Franklin D. Roosevelt, Winston Churchill, and Joseph Stalin met in Tehran to plan the Allied invasion of Europe, Niebuhr started thinking about his upcoming Raymond F. West Lectures at Stanford University, to be delivered in January. Earlier that year he had published the second volume of his masterwork, *The Nature and Destiny of Man*, which was based on his Gifford Lectures of 1939. Chapter 9 of this work, "The Kingdom of God and the Struggle for Justice," developed a vintage Niebuhr dialectic, arguing that the struggle for justice is even more revealing of the possibilities and limits of human powers than the quest for truth. The relationship of the kingdom of God to history is inescapably paradoxical, Niebuhr contended. History moves toward the realization of the kingdom, yet every occasion of its realization falls under divine judgment.[1]

This argument was the seed of *The Children of Light and the Children of Darkness*, the first draft of which Niebuhr delivered at Stanford. By then he realized that he was sketching his political philosophy. The following summer, while Allied forces launched D-Day and Operation Overload, he expanded the lectures into a book.

The Children of Light and the Children of Darkness offered a reconsideration of the side of Niebuhr's thought that he had previously considered to be firmly established. In the 1930s Niebuhr had featured his hard-edged politics and struggled to define his theology. By the early 1940s he had developed his theological perspective and was beginning to waver about his politics. The book that launched Niebuhr's fame, *Moral Man and Immoral Society* (1932), wedded his forcefully argued Socialism to a vague theology that denounced liberal theology while taking much of it for granted. Niebuhr spent the rest of the decade figuring out his theology, which meant, in his case, deepening his debt to Augustine and John Calvin. The Gifford Lectures revealed that he had arrived at Niebuhrian theology.

Meanwhile his politics were changing. Niebuhr was still an ardent state Socialist when he delivered the Gifford Lectures. He wanted state planners to replicate the pricing decisions of markets and government planners or guild organizations to organize an economy not linked by markets. By the early 1940s, however, Niebuhr had pragmatic reasons to pull back on his Socialism. If Roosevelt could enact most of the Socialist Party platform in two years, what was the point of sticking with the Socialist Party? More important, Niebuhr's Socialism had been focused on the equality principle, but by the early 1940s he realized that a realistic struggle for justice had to give at least equal priority to order and freedom. Moreover, in 1940 the Socialist Party in the United States opposed American intervention in the war in Europe. Niebuhr resigned from the party that year.

Some readers of this book, if they are like my students, will be jarred by Niebuhr's frequent charge of stupidity, which he leveled against utilitarians, liberals, German Romantics, Marxists, "other stupid children of light," and modern democratic theory as a whole. The early and middle Niebuhr had a penchant for personal polemic that the later Niebuhr found embarrassing. Niebuhr started in the early 1930s to call people that he disagreed with "stupid," but the irony of doing so was more apparent in his writings of that period than in *The Children of Light and the Children of Darkness*. In *Moral Man and Immoral Society*, Niebuhr adopted "stupid" as his favorite epithet, followed closely by "naïve," because he had set himself against liberal idealism, pacifism, *and* rationalism. Niebuhr enjoyed the irony of charging that liberal rationalists, besides being naïve, were not all that smart either.

Moral Man and Immoral Society established the tropes that Niebuhr invoked for the rest of his career. With an icy and aggressive tone, he admonished that politics is always about struggling for power. Human groups never willingly subordinate their interests to the interests of others. Morality belongs to the sphere of individual action, Niebuhr argued. On occasion, individuals rise above self-interest, motivated by compassion or love, but groups never overcome the power of self-interest and collective egotism that sustains their existence. For this reason the appeals to reason by secular liberals like John Dewey, and the appeals to reason and Christian love by Social Gospel liberals, were maddeningly stupid.

Niebuhr seethed at the ravages of the Great Depression, and he deplored the American aversion to Socialism. *Moral Man and Immoral Society* contended that history would either move forward to revolutionary Socialism or backward to fascist barbarism. There was no third way; the New Deal was a Band-Aid for a dying patient, capitalism. American Christianity needed to regain a sense of the tragedy of life, Niebuhr implored. The historical sweep of human life always reflects the predatory world of nature. In the private world of home and family, Niebuhr urged, love is the highest norm, but in the public world of groups and clashing interests, justice is the highest norm. In 1932, the dream of perfect justice was a dangerous illusion, because it encouraged fanaticism, but it was also "very valuable," because no justice was attainable if the hope of its perfect realization did not generate "a sublime madness in the soul."[2]

Moral Man and Immoral Society, the most important American theological work of the twentieth century, got terrible reviews. Liberal Protestant leaders howled at its hard-edged Marxism, its condemnations of liberal stupidity, and the fact that Niebuhr ignored the teachings of Jesus, had no theology of the church, and seemed to regard his lack of faith in God's regenerative power as a virtue. The book might be some kind of revolutionary realism, but how was it Christian?

Niebuhr realized that he had to formulate a better answer to this question for others and himself.
Thus he spent the 1930s revamping his theological
position—a neoliberal version of Reformed theology that treated the basic doctrines of Christianity as
"true myths." In *Reflections on the End of an Era* (1934),
Niebuhr ramped up his Marxist rhetoric, yet in the
book's closing pages he reclaimed the language of divine providence and grace. Thereafter Niebuhr drew
more and more deeply on Augustine, Martin Luther,
and John Calvin, refashioning the Augustinian and
Reformed theology of sin, redemption, and grace,
and addressing the problem of Jesus.[3]

Jesus taught an ethic of love perfectionism that paid
no attention to social consequences, Niebuhr argued.
Jesus did not concern himself with proximate ends,
using power responsibly, attaining justice, or defending it. Since Jesus merely asserted a religious ideal, his
teaching had no relevance to problems in the sphere of
politics, except for establishing the ideal. Niebuhr said
it plainly in *An Interpretation of Christian Ethics* (1935):
Jesus was no help with the problems of social ethics,
except in establishing an impossible ethical ideal that
defines gospel religion—the love-your-enemies ethical
perfectionism of the way of the cross. Religiously, for
Niebuhr, the cross was a symbol of God's judgment
on human sin and God's loving forgiveness; ethically,

it was a symbol of the importance and unattainability of the law of love.[4]

For Niebuhr, the heart of Christianity was a promise of deliverance from humanity's enslaving egotism through divine grace. God's grace saves sinful egotists by enabling them to surrender their prideful attempts to master their existence. *The Nature and Destiny of Man* worked this theme at length, laying the religious foundation of Niebuhr's realism—that the image of God in every human being is marred by selfishness and will-to-power. The human spirit finds a home and grasps a bit of its freedom in God's transcendence, where it also finds the limit of its freedom, a divine judgment upon the self's sinfulness, and the mercy that makes judgment bearable.

This was the theological foundation of *The Children of Light and the Children of Darkness*, though Niebuhr did not spell it out, only noting in the foreword to the first edition that his Christian worldview *was* his foundation. His recent writings about politics, collected in *Christianity and Power Politics* (1940), had been devoted to issues concerning the war. Before that, he had poured out a stream of political writings, many of which he no longer agreed with. *The Children of Light and the Children of Darkness* was a course correction and a plea for liberal renewal based on Niebuhr's participation in the Union for Democratic Action.[5]

Niebuhr had not spent the 1930s, as some have argued, urging the United States to arm for a battle against fascism. Rather, he had asked Americans to refrain from isolationism, to pay attention to the evils of fascism in Germany, Spain, and Italy, and to be aware of the need to resist fascism's expansion. In 1937 Niebuhr had condemned Roosevelt's naval buildup as a "sinister" evil, declaring that it had to be "resisted at all costs." The next year he blasted Roosevelt's billion-dollar defense budget as "the worst piece of militarism in modern history." Right up until the Munich crisis of September 1938, Niebuhr argued that the best way to avoid war was not to prepare for one; collective security was the realistic alternative to war. He supported passage of the Neutrality Acts of 1935 and 1937 and wanted the United States voluntarily to support League of Nations sanctions against Italy in 1935.[6]

The fact that even Reinhold Niebuhr stridently opposed Roosevelt's preparations to fight overseas is a measure of the revulsion for war that his generation felt after World War I. Niebuhr resisted his own lesser-evil rationale for war until Hitler's determination to conquer Europe became undeniable. Then Niebuhr campaigned to persuade Americans to smash fascist tyranny—and in so doing he became the foremost American theologian of the twentieth century.

The Children of Light and the Children of Darkness revealed that Niebuhr had dispensed with his Marxist "either/or" about history going forward or backward only. His new dialectic, expressed in the book's title, took up the timely question of how democracy should be defended. Modern American liberals were spiritual cousins of John Locke, Adam Smith, Jean-Jacques Rousseau, Thomas Paine, Jeremy Bentham, William Godwin, Johann G. Fichte, G. W. F. Hegel, and all true-believing Marxists, Niebuhr argued. All were "children of light" who believed that the conflict between self-interest and the general interest could be readily resolved. Locke's social contract, Smith's harmonizing invisible hand, and Rousseau's general will had so much confidence in reason or nature that only minimal social restraints on human egotism were needed. Fichte and Hegel actually believed that philosophy could synthesize the national and universal interests. Marxists even believed that no state would be necessary after the proletarian revolution occurred.

To their credit, Niebuhr acknowledged, most children of light recognized the existence of a moral law beyond themselves, although some of them called it something else. But all were naïve about the power of self-interest in society. This naïveté yielded bad arguments for democracy and made the children of light inept at defending democracy against "children of darkness."

The children of darkness were wise and strong in their moral cynicism, Niebuhr warned. They understood self-interest terribly well and were not constrained by a moral law beyond themselves. Hobbes and Machiavelli were children of darkness, showing that realism lacking a moral dimension is toxic and corrupting. The showcase example, "Nazi barbarism," had plunged Europe into total war. If it was possible for a force of such "demonic fury" to arise in the twentieth century, Niebuhr argued, the classic liberal picture of a harmless, essentially individualistic social existence was refuted. In 1944, Niebuhr had many New York Socialist friends who saw little difference between the barbarity of Nazi fascism and Soviet Communism, but Niebuhr settled for a wartime evasion, mindful that American newsmagazines called Stalin "Uncle Joe." It was too soon to place Stalin unequivocally among the children of darkness, Niebuhr suggested, but down the road, "Stalin will probably have the same relation to the early dreamers of the Marxist dreams which Napoleon has to the liberal dreamers of the eighteenth century."[7]

Modern liberals thought that democracy fulfilled an ideal that people deserved on account of their moral worth. The children of darkness, being cunning and immoral in their pursuit of power, better understood the centrality of will-to-power in politics and history. This dialectic yielded Niebuhr's most famous epigram: "Man's capacity for justice makes democracy possible, but man's inclination to injustice makes democracy necessary." Liberal democracy is worth defending, not because it fulfills a moral ideal or because modern civilized types deserve nothing less, but because it is the best way to restrain human egotism and will-to-power.[8]

In 1944, Niebuhr still believed that this argument for political democracy extended to economic democracy. If political democracy did not lead to significant gains in worker, community, and social ownership, the capitalist class would end up owning the political system, thus subverting democracy. Democracy was needed in the economic sphere as a brake on the overweening greed and will-to-domination of the capitalist class, Niebuhr argued: "Since economic power, as every other form of social power, is a defensive force when possessed in moderation and a temptation to injustice when it is great enough to give the agent power over others, it would seem that its widest and most equitable distribution would make for the highest degree of justice."[9]

"It would seem" was a retreat, however. Niebuhr still believed in economic democracy as an ideal, even that it was essential to social justice. But he no longer believed it was possible in his country. Having ridiculed the New Deal while it was being built, he made his peace with it, settling for a trinity of countervailing powers: big business, big labor, and big government. This was a strategy for progressive renewal, he insisted. Gradual experimentation and reform would get the right balance among the three economic powers. The property issue is never really solved; it must be continually negotiated within democracy, which is a method of finding proximate solutions for problems that cannot be solved.

Upon completing the manuscript of *The Children of Light* in August 1944, Niebuhr took a semester leave from Union Theological Seminary to campaign for the newly founded Liberal Party of New York and to raise funds for the UDA. For fifteen years he had dreamed of building a party in which intellectuals and labor leaders worked together for progressive change. Niebuhr worked tirelessly for the UDA, undertaking extensive speaking tours on its behalf. The UDA was the closest that he came to fulfilling his dream after he resigned from the Socialist Party. *The Children of Light and the Children of Darkness*, in its context, was about Niebuhr's activism in the UDA and his hope for it.

In 1947 the UDA morphed into the Americans for Democratic Action, a powerhouse advocacy organization of the Democratic Party's left wing. *The Children of Light and the Children of Darkness*, it turned out, was about something vastly larger than the UDA.

It became the rationale for the "Vital Center" liberals who in 1948 became so influential in the Democratic Party.

Reinhold Niebuhr, for better and for worse, did not question whether his preoccupation with government politics was appropriate for a Christian theologian. He did question, however, whether his trademark dichotomy between love and justice adequately represented love or justice, or the relation between them. In the 1930s Niebuhr equated justice with equality, or an equal balance of power, and he blasted everyone who tried to get a social ethic out of Jesus. Always he admonished that Jesus was no help with problems of proximate means and ends, necessary violence, and calculated consequences.

But Niebuhr realized that something was missing in his stark dichotomizing between love and justice. The very thing that kept him and others in the struggle for justice, whether or not they succeeded, was the love ethic. *That* was its social relevance. Love is not merely the content of an impossible ethical ideal. It is the motive force of the struggle for justice.

The Nature and Destiny of Man, grasping the difference, introduced a relational view of justice. *The Children of Light and the Children of Darkness* expanded upon it. Subsequently, Niebuhr asked readers to judge him by his later works in this area, not by his works of the 1930s, when he was "only dimly feeling [his] way." The later Niebuhr conceived justice as a relational term that depends on the force of love and that cannot be defined abstractly. There are no definitive principles of justice, for all such instruments are too corrupt to be definitive. But Niebuhr argued that three regulative principles are useful: equality, freedom, and order. Social justice is an application of the law of love to the sociopolitical sphere, and love is the motivating energy of the struggle for justice. The meaning of justice cannot be taken directly from the principles. It is determined only in the interaction of love and situation, through the mediation of the principles of equality, freedom, and order.[10]

Niebuhr had a method for attaining proximate gains toward justice, though he had no theory of justice. He was the greatest American theologian of the twentieth century, though he took no interest in the finer points of doctrine. To read almost anything that he wrote, it helps to have a high threshold for ambiguity and paradox. For Niebuhr, the love ethic of Jesus, despite its idealism and also because of it, was always the point, the motive, and the end, even when it had no concrete social meaning. Since Niebuhr followed Jesus, he had to take up responsibility for society's problems, even if Jesus did not. Love is uncalculating concern for the dignity of persons, and thus it asserts no interests, but inasmuch as love motivates concern for the dignity of persons, it also motivates a passion for justice overflowing with interests and requiring principles of justice.

Niebuhr spent his career sorting out these paradoxes. Some of his allies, dubbing themselves "atheists for Niebuhr," treated Niebuhr's theology as a dispensable vestige of his ethical realism. Niebuhr took delight in his secular following, but for him, the religious part of Christian realism was indispensable, because without it history had no meaning and there was no reason to believe that history leads anywhere. *The Children of Light and the Children of Darkness*, one of Niebuhr's more secular books, put it emphatically: faith in the existence of a divine power is "indispensable" to the historical struggle for a just order, for "without it we are driven to alternative moods of sentimentality and despair."[11]

Today Niebuhr's name is back in public discussion mostly because the Bush Administration pitched realism aside on the way to invading Iraq, after which Barack Obama, campaigning for president, told an interviewer that Niebuhr was his favorite political thinker. There are many kinds of Niebuhrians, to whom Niebuhr symbolizes different things in theology, ethics, and politics. But a few things are central to his legacy regardless of the view that one takes concerning Niebuhr's method, orthodoxy, ecclesiology, Cold War militarism, patriotic nationalism, Euro-American purview, views on racial and gender justice, or other usual topics of debate.

Niebuhr symbolizes the possibility of a prudent liberalism that takes the measure of every group's self-interest and is chastened by a realistic understanding of the limits of power. He is the symbol of the very attempt to fuse Christian ethics and political realism. He is the most important thinker of the past century concerning the relation of Christianity to problems of social ethics and politics. And his great theme, the necessity of navigating between sentimental idealism and cynical realism, is nowhere addressed more insightfully than in *The Children of Light and the Children of Darkness*.

GARY DORRIEN

Reinhold Niebuhr Professor of Social Ethics, Union Theological Seminary
Professor of Religion, Columbia University

1. Reinhold Niebuhr, *The Nature and Destiny of Man*, 2 vols. (New York: Charles Scribner's Sons, 1941–43), 244–86. This introduction contains arguments that I have made in Gary Dorrien, *The Making of American Liberal Theology: Idealism, Realism, and Modernity, 1900–1950* (Louisville, KY: Westminster John Knox Press, 2003), 435–89; Dorrien, *Social Ethics in the Making: Interpreting an American Tradition* (Oxford: Wiley-Blackwell, 2009), 226–94; and Dorrien, *Economy, Difference, Empire: Social Ethics for Social Justice* (New York: Columbia University Press, 2010), 29–65.

2. Reinhold Niebuhr, *Moral Man and Immoral Society: A Study in Ethics and Politics* (New York: Charles Scribner's Sons, 1932), 277.

3. Reinhold Niebuhr, *Reflections on the End of an Era* (New York: Charles Scribner's Sons, 1934).

4. Reinhold Niebuhr, *An Interpretation of Christian Ethics* (New York: Charles Scribner's Sons, 1935).

5. Reinhold Niebuhr, *Christianity and Power Politics* (New York: Charles Scribner's Sons, 1940).

6. Reinhold Niebuhr, "Brief Comments," *Radical Religion* 3 (Winter 1937): 7; Niebuhr, "Brief Notes," *Radical Religion* 3 (Spring 1938): 7; see also Niebuhr, "European Impressions," *Radical Religion* 2 (Fall 1937): 31–33.

7. Reinhold Niebuhr, *The Children of Light and the Children of Darkness* (New York: Charles Scribner's Sons, 1944): 23, 33.

8. Ibid., xi.

9. Ibid., 113–14; see Reinhold Niebuhr, "The Creed of Modern Christian Socialists," *Radical Religion* 3 (Spring 1938): 16.

10. Reinhold Niebuhr, "Reply to Interpretation and Criticism," in *Reinhold Niebuhr: His Religious, Social, and Political Thought*, ed. Charles W. Kegley and Robert W. Bretall (New York: Macmillan, 1956), 434; see also Niebuhr, *The Nature and Destiny of Man*, vol. 2, 246–69; Niebuhr, "Justice and Love," *Christianity and Society* (Fall 1950), reprinted in Niebuhr, *Love and Justice: Selections from the Shorter Writings of Reinhold Niebuhr*, ed. D. B. Robertson (Philadelphia: Westminster Press, 1957), 27–29; Niebuhr, *Faith and History: A Comparison of Christian and Modern Views of History* (New York: Charles Scribner's Sons, 1949), 171–95.

11. Niebuhr, *The Children of Light and the Children of Darkness*, 189

THE pace of modern history is so rapid, that events have overtaken and rendered obsolete some of the occasional references in this volume of political philosophy first published fifteen years ago. I do not think that they have refuted the central thesis of the book, which is that a free society prospers best in a cultural, religious and moral atmosphere which encourages neither a too pessimistic nor too optimistic view of human nature. Both moral sentimentality in politics and moral pessimism encourage totalitarian regimes, the one because it encourages the opinion that it is not necessary to check the power of government, and the second because it believes that only absolute political authority can restrain the anarchy, created by conflicting and competitive interests.

But the occasional and dated judgments which I allowed myself fifteen years ago obviously need revision. For instance China is not "potentially" but actually a great power. America does not oscillate between isolationism and responsibility. The undoubted power, with which we emerged after the second world war has put an end to our isolationist impulses. We are now a great hegemonous nation in the non-communist world and our problem is to exercise the responsibilities, concomitant with power, without the moral sentimentality or pretension, which have characterized our national life from the days of our innocency. We have accepted the responsibilities but we are still inclined to pretend that our power is exercised by a peculiarly virtuous nation. The uniqueness of our virtue is questioned both by our friends and our enemies. All historic virtues and achievements are more ambiguous and fragmentary, than we are inclined to believe.

I would not want to change the basic presupposition of the final chapter on integrating the world community. The failure to reach accord with the communists on any important matters proves that a rational accommodation of competing interests in a community, whether national or global, is still more difficult than our idealists have consistently assumed. But meanwhile we live in a new dimension of history, created by the "cold war" on the one hand and the absolute impossibility of resorting to a nuclear war on the other. Everything said in the last chapter, which does not weigh this absolutely unpredicted dimension of the problem is therefore dated. We now know that we must arrange a tolerable co-existence with a resolute foe, the alternative being mutual annihilation. I confess without undue shame that I was not sufficiently prescient fifteen years ago to anticipate the creative and destructive possibilities inherent in the nuclear stalemate, which prevents a shooting war but which also offers no easy path to world community. If we escape disaster it will only be by the slow growth of mutual trust and tissues of community over the awful chasm of the present international tension.

October, 1959.   REINHOLD NIEBUHR

FOREWORD TO THE FIRST EDITION

THE substance of this volume was presented in a series of lectures on the Raymond W. West Memorial Foundation at Leland Stanford University, Palo Alto, California, in January 1944. It has been considerably expanded, since delivery of the lectures, in preparing them for publication.

The Raymond F. West Memorial Lectures on Immortality, Human Conduct, and Human Destiny were established at Leland Stanford University in 1910 by Mr. and Mrs. Frederick W. West of Seattle in memory of their son, a member of the class of 1906, who died before the completion of his college course. These lectures were the fifteenth in the history of the foundation.

I desire to express my gratitude to the faculty and students of the university for the sympathetic understanding which they brought to the thesis of the lectures and with which they received my exposition of the thesis. I owe special gratitude to Professor Edgar E. Robinson, head of the history department of the university, and Mrs. Robinson and to the chaplain of the university, Professor D. Elton Trueblood and Mrs. Trueblood for their great kindness to me during my Stanford visit.

The thesis of this volume grew out of my conviction that democracy has a more compelling justification and requires a more realistic vindication than is given it by the liberal culture with which it has been associated in modern history. The excessively optimistic estimates of human nature and of human history with which the democratic credo has been historically associated are a source of peril to democratic society; for contemporary experience is refuting this optimism and there is danger that it will seem to refute the democratic ideal as well.

A free society requires some confidence in the ability of men to reach tentative and tolerable adjustments between their competing interests and to arrive at some common notions of justice which transcend all partial interests. A consistent pessimism in regard to man's rational capacity for justice invariably leads to absolutistic political theories; for they prompt the conviction that only preponderant power can coerce the various vitalities of a community into a working harmony. But a too consistent optimism in regard to man's ability and inclination to grant justice to his fellows obscures the perils of chaos which perennially confront every society, including a free society. In one sense a democratic society is particularly exposed to the dangers of confusion. If these perils are not appreciated they may overtake a free society and invite the alternative evil of tyranny.

But modern democracy requires a more realistic philosophical and religious basis, not only in order to anticipate and understand the perils to which it is exposed; but also to give it a more persuasive justification. Man's capacity for justice makes democracy possible; but man's inclination to injustice makes democracy necessary. In all nondemocratic political theories the state or the ruler is invested with uncontrolled power for the sake of achieving order and unity in the community. But the pessimism which prompts and justifies this policy is not consistent; for it is not applied, as it should be, to the ruler. If men are inclined to deal unjustly with their fellows, the possession of power aggravates this inclination. That is why irresponsible and uncontrolled power is the greatest source of injustice.

The democratic techniques of a free society place checks upon the power of the ruler and administrator and thus prevent it from becoming vexatious. The perils of uncontrolled power are perennial reminders of the virtues of a democratic society; particularly if a society should become inclined to impatience with the dangers of freedom and should be tempted to choose the advantages of coerced unity at the price of freedom.

The consistent optimism of our liberal culture has prevented modern democratic societies both from gauging the perils of freedom accurately and from appreciating democracy fully as the only alternative to injustice and oppression. When this optimism is not qualified to accord with the real and complex facts of human nature and history, there is always a danger that sentimentality will give way to despair and that a too consistent optimism will alternate with a too consistent pessimism.

I have not sought to elaborate the religious and theological convictions upon which the political philosophy of the following pages rests. It will be apparent, however, that they are informed by the belief that a Christian view of human nature is more adequate for the development of a democratic society than either the optimism with which democracy has become historically associated or the moral cynicism which inclines human communities to tyrannical political strategies.

REINHOLD NIEBUHR

August, 1944.

CHAPTER ONE

THE CHILDREN OF LIGHT AND THE CHILDREN OF DARKNESS

I

DEMOCRACY, as every other historic ideal and institution, contains both ephemeral and more permanently valid elements. Democracy is on the one hand the characteristic fruit of a bourgeois civilization; on the other hand it is a perennially valuable form of social organization in which freedom and order are made to support, and not to contradict, each other.

Democracy is a "bourgeois ideology" in so far as it expresses the typical viewpoints of the middle classes who have risen to power in European civilization in the past three or four centuries. Most of the democratic ideals, as we know them, were weapons of the commercial classes who engaged in stubborn, and ultimately victorious, conflict with the ecclesiastical and aristocratic rulers of the

I

feudal-medieval world. The ideal of equality, unknown in the democratic life of the Greek city states and derived partly from Christian and partly from Stoic sources, gave the bourgeois classes a sense of self-respect in overcoming the aristocratic pretension and condescension of the feudal overlords of medieval society. The middle classes defeated the combination of economic and political power of mercantilism by stressing economic liberty; and, through the principles of political liberty, they added the political power of suffrage to their growing economic power. The implicit assumptions, as well as the explicit ideals, of democratic civilization were also largely the fruit of middle-class existence. The social and historical optimism of democratic life, for instance, represents the typical illusion of an advancing class which mistook its own progress for the progress of the world.

Since bourgeois civilization, which came to birth in the sixteenth to eighteenth centuries and reached its zenith in the nineteenth century, is now obviously in grave peril, if not actually in *rigor mortis* in the twentieth century, it must be obvious that democracy, in so far as it is a middle-class ideology, also faces its doom.

This fate of democracy might be viewed with equanimity, but for the fact that it has a deeper dimension and broader validity than its middle-class character. Ideally democracy is a permanently valid form of social and political organization which does justice to two dimensions of human existence: to man's spiritual stature and his social character; to the uniqueness and variety of life, as well as to the common necessities of all men. Bourgeois democracy frequently exalted the individual at the expense of the community; but its emphasis upon liberty contained a valid element, which transcended its excessive individualism. The community requires liberty as much as does the individual; and the individual requires community more than bourgeois thought comprehended. Democracy can therefore not be equated with freedom. An ideal democratic order seeks unity within the conditions of freedom; and maintains freedom within the framework of order.

Man requires freedom in his social organization because he is "essentially" free, which is to say, that he has the capacity for indeterminate transcendence over the processes and limitations of nature. This freedom enables him to make history and to elaborate communal organizations in boundless variety and in endless breadth and extent. But he also requires community because he is by nature social. He cannot fulfill his life within himself but only in responsible and mutual relations with his fellows.

Bourgeois democrats are inclined to believe that freedom is primarily a necessity for the individual, and that community and social order are necessary only because there are many individuals in a small world, so that minimal restrictions are required to prevent confusion. Actually the community requires freedom as much as the individual; and the individual requires order as much as does the community.

Both the individual and the community require freedom so that neither communal nor historical restraints may prematurely arrest the potencies which inhere in man's essential freedom and which express themselves collectively as well as individually. It is true that individuals are usually the initiators of new insights and the proponents of novel methods. Yet there are collective forces at work in society which are not the conscious contrivance of individuals. In any event society is as much the beneficiary of freedom as the individual. In a free society new forces may enter into competition with the old and gradually establish themselves. In a traditional or tyrannical form of social organization new forces are either suppressed, or they establish themselves at the price of social convulsion and upheaval.

The order of a community is, on the other hand, a boon to the individual as well as to the community. The individual cannot be a true self in isolation. Nor can he live within the confines of the community which "nature" establishes in the minimal cohesion of family and herd. His freedom transcends these limits of nature, and therefore makes larger and larger social units both possible and necessary. It is precisely because of the essential freedom of man that he requires a contrived order in his community.

The democratic ideal is thus more valid than the libertarian and individualistic version of it which bourgeois civilization elaborated. Since the bourgeois version has been discredited by the events of contemporary history and since, in any event, bourgeois civilization is in process of disintegration, it becomes important to distinguish and save what is permanently valid from what is ephemeral in the democratic order.

If democracy is to survive it must find a more

adequate cultural basis than the philosophy which has informed the building of the bourgeois world. The inadequacy of the presuppositions upon which the democratic experiment rests does not consist merely in the excessive individualism and libertarianism of the bourgeois world view; though it must be noted that this excessive individualism prompted a civil war in the whole western world in which the rising proletarian classes pitted an excessive collectivism against the false individualism of middle-class life. This civil conflict contributed to the weakness of democratic civilization when faced with the threat of barbarism. Neither the individualism nor the collectivism did justice to all the requirements of man's social life, and the conflict between half-truth and half-truth divided the civilized world in such a way that the barbarians were able to claim first one side and then the other in this civil conflict as their provisional allies.[1]

But there is a more fundamental error in the social philosophy of democratic civilization than

---

[1]The success of Nazi diplomacy and propaganda in claiming the poor in democratic civilization as their allies against the "plutocrats" in one moment, and in the next seeking to ally the privileged classes in their battle against "communism," is a nice indication of the part which the civil war in democratic civilization played in allowing barbarism to come so near to a triumph over civilization.

the individualism of bourgeois democracy and the collectivism of Marxism. It is the confidence of both bourgeois and proletarian idealists in the possibility of achieving an easy resolution of the tension and conflict between self-interest and the general interest. Modern bourgeois civilization is not, as Catholic philosophers and medievalists generally assert, a rebellion against universal law, or a defiance of universal standards of justice, or a war against the historic institutions which sought to achieve and preserve some general social and international harmony. Modern secularism is not, as religious idealists usually aver, merely a rationalization of self-interest, either individual or collective. Bourgeois individualism may be excessive and it may destroy the individual's organic relation to the community; but it was not intended to destroy either the national or the international order. On the contrary the social idealism which informs our democratic civilization had a touching faith in the possibility of achieving a simple harmony between self-interest and the general welfare on every level.

It is not true that Nazism is the final fruit of a moral cynicism which had its rise in the Renaissance and Reformation, as Catholic apologists aver. Nazi barbarism is the final fruit of a moral cynicism which was only a subordinate note in the cultural life of the modern period, and which remained subordinate until very recently. Modern civilization did indeed seek to give the individual a greater freedom in the national community than the traditional feudal order had given him; and it did seek to free the nations of restraints placed upon their freedom by the international church. But it never cynically defied the general interest in the name of self-interest, either individual or collective. It came closer to doing this nationally than individually. Machiavelli's amoral "Prince," who knows no law beyond his own will and power, is made to bear the whole burden of the Catholic polemic against the modern world. It must be admitted that Machiavelli is the first of a long line of moral cynics in the field of international relations. But this moral cynicism only qualifies, and does not efface, the general universalistic overtone of modern liberal idealism. In the field of domestic politics the war of uncontrolled interests may have been the consequence, but it was certainly not the intention, of middle-class individualists. Nor was the conflict between nations in our modern world their intention. They did demand a greater degree of freedom for the nations; but they believed that it was possible to achieve an uncontrolled harmony between them, once the allegedly irrelevant restrictions of the old religio-political order were removed. In this they proved to be mistaken. They did not make the mistake, however, of giving simple moral sanction to self-interest. They depended rather upon controls and restraints which proved to be inadequate.

II

In illumining this important distinction more fully, we may well designate the moral cynics, who know no law beyond their will and interest, with a scriptural designation of "children of this world" or "children of darkness." Those who believe that self-interest should be brought under the discipline of a higher law could then be termed "the children of light." This is no mere arbitrary device; for evil is always the assertion of some self-interest without regard to the whole, whether the whole be conceived as the immediate community, or the total community of mankind, or the total order of the world. The good is, on the other hand, always the harmony of the whole on various levels. Devotion to a subordinate and premature "whole" such as the nation, may of course become evil, viewed from the perspective of a larger whole, such as the community of mankind. The "children of light" may thus be defined as those who seek to bring self-interest under the discipline of a more universal law and in harmony with a more universal good.

According to the scripture "the children of this world are in their generation wiser than the children of light." This observation fits the modern situation. Our democratic civilization has been built, not by children of darkness but by foolish children of light. It has been under attack by the children of darkness, by the moral cynics, who declare that a strong nation need acknowledge no law beyond its strength. It has come close to complete disaster under this attack, not because it accepted the same creed as the cynics; but because it underestimated the power of self-interest, both individual and collective, in modern society. The children of light have not been as wise as the children of darkness.

The children of darkness are evil because they know no law beyond the self. They are wise, though evil, because they understand the power of self-interest. The children of light are virtuous because they have some conception of a higher law than their own will. They are usually foolish because they do not know the power of self-will. They underestimate the peril of anarchy in both the national and the international community. Modern democratic civilization is, in short, sentimental rather than cynical. It has an easy solution for the problem of anarchy and chaos on both the national and international level of community, because of its fatuous and superficial view of man. It does not know that the same man who is ostensibly devoted to the "common good" may have desires and ambitions, hopes and fears, which set him at variance with his neighbor.

It must be understood that the children of light are foolish not merely because they underestimate the power of self-interest among the children of darkness. They underestimate this power among themselves. The democratic world came so close to disaster not merely because it never believed that Nazism possessed the demonic fury which it avowed. Civilization refused to recognize the power of class interest in its own communities. It also spoke glibly of an international conscience; but the children of darkness meanwhile skilfully set nation against nation. They were thereby enabled to despoil one nation after another, without every civilized nation coming to the defence of each. Moral cynicism had a provisional advantage over moral sentimentality. Its advantage lay not merely in its own lack of moral scruple but also in its shrewd assessment of the power of self-interest, individual and national, among the children of light, despite their moral protestations.

While our modern children of light, the secularized idealists, were particularly foolish and blind, the more "Christian" children of light have been almost equally guilty of this error. Modern liberal Protestantism was probably even more sentimental in its appraisal of the moral realities in our political life than secular idealism, and Catholicism could see nothing but cynical rebellion in the modern secular revolt against Catholic universalism and a Catholic "Christian" civilization. In Catholic thought medieval political universalism is always accepted at face value. Rebellion against medieval culture is therefore invariably regarded as the fruit of moral cynicism. Actually the middle-class revolt against the feudal order was partially prompted by a generous idealism, not unmixed of course with peculiar middle-class interests. The feudal order was not so simply a Christian civilization as Catholic defenders of it aver. It compounded its devotion to a universal order with the special interests of the priestly and aristocratic bearers of effective social power. The rationalization of their unique position in the feudal order may not have been more marked than the subsequent rationalization of bourgeois interests in the liberal world. But it is idle to deny this "ideological taint" in the feudal order and to pretend that rebels against the order were merely rebels against order as such. They were rebels against a particular order which gave an undue advantage to the aristocratic opponents of the middle classes.[2] The blindness of Catholicism to its own ideological taint is typical of the blindness of the children of light.

---

[2] John of Salisbury expresses a quite perfect rationalization of clerical political authority in his *Policraticus* in the twelfth century. He writes: "Those who preside over the practice of religion should be looked up to and venerated as the soul of the body. . . . Furthermore since the soul is, as it were, the prince of the body and has a rule over the whole thereof, so those whom our author calls the prefects of religion preside over the entire body." Book V, ch. ii.

A modern Catholic historian accepts this justification of clerical rule at its face value as he speaks of Machiavelli's politics as a "total assault upon the principles of men like John of Salisbury, preferring to the goodness of Christ, the stamina of Cæsar." (Emmet John Hughes, *The Church and the Liberal Society*, p. 33.)

John of Salisbury's political principles were undoubtedly more moral than Machiavelli's. But the simple identification of his justification of clericalism with the "goodness of Christ" is a nice illustration of the blindness of the children of light, whether Christian or secular.

Our modern civilization, as a middle-class revolt against an aristocratic and clerical order, was irreligious partly because a Catholic civilization had so compounded the eternal sanctities with the contingent and relative justice and injustice of an agrarian-feudal order, that the new and dynamic bourgeois social force was compelled to challenge not only the political-economic arrangements of the order but also the eternal sanctities which hallowed it.

If modern civilization represents a bourgeois revolt against feudalism, modern culture represents the revolt of new thought, informed by modern science, against a culture in which religious authority had fixed premature and too narrow limits for the expansion of science and had sought to restrain the curiosity of the human mind from inquiring into "secondary causes." The culture which venerated science in place of religion, worshipped natural causation in place of God, and which regarded the cool prudence of bourgeois man as morally more normative than Christian love, has proved itself to be less profound than it appeared to be in the seventeenth and eighteenth centuries. But these inadequacies, which must be further examined as typical of the foolishness of modern children of light, do not validate the judgment that these modern rebels were really children of darkness, intent upon defying the truth or destroying universal order.

The modern revolt against the feudal order and the medieval culture was occasioned by the assertion of new vitalities in the social order and the discovery of new dimensions in the cultural enterprise of mankind. It was truly democratic in so far as it challenged the premature and tentative unity of a society and the stabilization of a culture, and in so far as it developed new social and cultural possibilities. The conflict between the middle classes and the aristocrats, between the scientists and the priests, was not a conflict between children of darkness and children of light. It was a conflict between pious and less pious children of light, both of whom were unconscious of the corruption of self-interest in all ideal achievements and pretensions of human culture.

III

In this conflict the devotees of medieval religion were largely unconscious of the corruption of self-interest in their own position; but it must be admitted that they were not as foolish as their secular successors in their estimate of the force of self-interest in human society. Catholicism did strive for an inner and religious discipline upon inordinate desire; and it had a statesmanlike conception of the necessity of legal and political restraint upon the power of egotism, both individual and collective, in the national and the more universal human community.

Our modern civilization, on the other hand, was ushered in on a wave of boundless social optimism. Modern secularism is divided into many schools. But all the various schools agreed in rejecting the Christian doctrine of original sin. It is not possible to explain the subtleties or to measure the profundity of this doctrine in this connection. But it is necessary to point out that the doctrine makes an important contribution to any adequate social and political theory the lack of which has robbed bourgeois theory of real wisdom; for it emphasizes a fact which every page of human history attests. Through it one may understand that no matter how wide the perspectives which the human mind may reach, how broad the loyalties which the human imagination may conceive, how universal the community which human statecraft may organize, or how pure the aspirations of the saintliest idealists may be, there is no level of human moral or social achievement in which there is not some corruption of inordinate self-love.

This sober and true view of the human situation was neatly rejected by modern culture. That is why it conceived so many fatuous and futile plans for resolving the conflict between the self and the community; and between the national and the world community. Whenever modern idealists are confronted with the divisive and corrosive effects of man's self-love, they look for some immediate cause of this perennial tendency, usually in some specific form of social organization. One school holds that men would be good if only political institutions would not corrupt them; another believes that they would be good if the prior evil of a faulty economic organization could be eliminated. Or another school thinks of this evil as no more than ignorance, and therefore waits for a more perfect educational process to redeem man from his partial and particular loyalties. But no school asks how it is that an essentially good man could have produced corrupting and tyrannical political organizations or exploiting economic organizations, or fanatical and superstitious religious organizations.

The result of this persistent blindness to the obvious and tragic facts of man's social history is that democracy has had to maintain itself precariously against the guile and the malice of the children of darkness, while its statesmen and guides conjured up all sorts of abstract and abortive plans for the creation of perfect national and international communities.

The confidence of modern secular idealism in the possibility of an easy resolution of the tension between individual and community, or between classes, races and nations is derived from a too optimistic view of human nature. This too generous estimate of human virtue is intimately related to an erroneous estimate of the dimensions of the human stature. The conception of human nature which underlies the social and political attitudes of a liberal democratic culture is that of an essentially harmless individual. The survival impulse, which man shares with the animals, is regarded as the normative form of his egoistic drive. If this were a true picture of the human situation man might be, or might become, as harmless as seventeenth- and eighteenth-century thought assumed. Unfortunately for the validity of this picture of man, the most significant distinction between the

human and the animal world is that the impulses
of the former are "spiritualized" in the human
world. Human capacities for evil as well as for
good are derived from this spiritualization. There
is of course always a natural survival impulse at
the core of all human ambition. But this survival
impulse cannot be neatly disentangled from two
forms of its spiritualization. The one form is the
desire to fulfill the potentialities of life and not
merely to maintain its existence. Man is the kind
of animal who cannot merely live. If he lives at
all he is bound to seek the realization of his true
nature; and to his true nature belongs his fulfillment in the lives of others. The will to live is thus
transmuted into the will to self-realization; and
self-realization involves self-giving in relations to
others. When this desire for self-realization is fully
explored it becomes apparent that it is subject to
the paradox that the highest form of self-realization is the consequence of self-giving, but that it
cannot be the intended consequence without being
prematurely limited. Thus the will to live is finally
transmuted into its opposite in the sense that only
in self-giving can the self be fulfilled, for: "He that
findeth his life shall lose it: and he that loseth his
life for my sake shall find it."[3]

[3]Matthew 10:39.

On the other hand the will-to-live is also spiritually transmuted into the will-to-power or into the desire for "power and glory." Man, being more than a natural creature, is not interested merely in physical survival but in prestige and social approval. Having the intelligence to anticipate the perils in which he stands in nature and history, he invariably seeks to gain security against these perils by enhancing his power, individually and collectively. Possessing a darkly unconscious sense of his insignificance in the total scheme of things, he seeks to compensate for his insignificance by pretensions of pride. The conflicts between men are thus never simple conflicts between competing survival impulses. They are conflicts in which each man or group seeks to guard its power and prestige against the peril of competing expressions of power and pride. Since the very possession of power and prestige always involves some encroachment upon the prestige and power of others, this conflict is by its very nature a more stubborn and difficult one than the mere competition between various survival impulses in nature. It remains to be added that this conflict expresses itself even more cruelly in collective than in individual terms. Human behaviour being less individualistic than secular liberalism assumed, the struggle between classes, races and other groups in human society is not as easily resolved by the expedient of dissolving the groups as liberal democratic idealists assumed.

Since the survival impulse in nature is transmuted into two different and contradictory spiritualized forms, which we may briefly designate as the will-to-live-truly and the will-to-power, man is at variance with himself. The power of the second impulse places him more fundamentally in conflict with his fellowman than democratic liberalism realizes. The fact he cannot realize himself, except in organic relation with his fellows, makes the community more important than bourgeois individualism understands. The fact that the two impulses, though standing in contradiction to each other, are also mixed and compounded with each other on every level of human life, makes the simple distinctions between good and evil, between selfishness and altruism, with which liberal idealism has tried to estimate moral and political facts, invalid. The fact that the will-to-power inevitably justifies itself in terms of the morally more acceptable will to realize man's true nature means that the egoistic corruption of universal ideals is a much more persistent fact in human conduct than any moralistic creed is inclined to admit.

If we survey any period of history, and not merely the present tragic era of world catastrophe, it becomes quite apparent that human ambitions, lusts and desires, are more inevitably inordinate, that both human creativity and human evil reach greater heights, and that conflicts in the community between varying conceptions of the good and between competing expressions of vitality are of more tragic proportions than was anticipated in the basic philosophy which underlies democratic civilization.

There is a specially ironic element in the effort of the seventeenth century to confine man to the limits of a harmless "nature" or to bring all his actions under the discipline of a cool prudence. For while democratic social philosophy was elaborating the picture of a harmless individual, moved by no more than a survival impulse, living in a social peace guaranteed by a pre-established harmony of nature, the advancing natural sciences were enabling man to harness the ·powers of nature, and to give his desires and ambitions a more limitless scope than they previously had. The

static inequalities of an agrarian society were transmuted into the dynamic inequalities of an industrial age. The temptation to inordinate expressions
of the possessive impulse, created by the new wealth
of a technical civilization, stood in curious and
ironic contradiction to the picture of essentially
moderate and ordinate desires which underlay the
social philosophy ·of the physiocrats and of Adam
Smith. Furthermore a technical society developed
new and more intensive forms of social cohesion
and a greater centralization of economic process in
defiance of the individualistic conception of social
relations which informed the liberal philosophy.[4]

The demonic fury of fascist politics in which a
collective will expresses boundless ambitions and
imperial desires and in which the instruments of
a technical civilization are used to arm this will
with a destructive power, previously unknown in
history, represents a melancholy historical refutation of the eighteenth- and nineteenth-century conceptions of a harmless and essentially individual

---

[4]Thus vast collective forms of "free enterprise," embodied
in monopolistic and large-scale financial and industrial institutions, still rationalize their desire for freedom from political
control in terms of a social philosophy which Adam Smith
elaborated for individuals. Smith was highly critical of the budding large-scale enterprise of his day and thought it ought to
be restricted to insurance companies and banks.

human life. Human desires are expressed more collectively, are less under the discipline of prudent calculation, and are more the masters of, and less limited by, natural forces than the democratic creed had understood.

While the fury of fascist politics represents a particularly vivid refutation of the democratic view of human nature, the developments within the confines of democratic civilization itself offer almost as telling a refutation. The liberal creed is never an explicit instrument of the children of darkness. But it is surprising to what degree the forces of darkness are able to make covert use of the creed. One must therefore, in analyzing the liberal hope of a simple social and political harmony, be equally aware of the universalistic presuppositions which underlie the hope and of the egoistic corruptions (both individual and collective) which inevitably express themselves in our culture in terms of, and in despite of, the creed. One must understand that it is· a creed of children of light; but also that it betrays their blindness to the forces of darkness.

In the social philosophy of Adam Smith there was both a religious guarantee of the preservation of community and a moral demand that the individual consider its claims. The religious guarantee was contained in Smith's secularized version of providence. Smith believed that when a man is guided by self-interest he is also "led by an invisible hand to promote an end which is not his intention."[5] This "invisible hand" is of course the power of a pre-established social harmony, conceived as a harmony of nature, which transmutes conflicts of self-interest into a vast scheme of mutual service.

Despite this determinism Smith does not hesitate to make moral demands upon men to sacrifice their interests to the wider interest. The universalistic presupposition which underlies Smith's thought is clearly indicated for instance in such an observation as this: "The wise and virtuous man is at all times willing that his own private interests should be sacrificed to the public interest of his own particular order of society—that the interests of this order of society be sacrificed to the greater interest of the state. He should therefore be equally willing that all those inferior interests should be sacrificed to the greater interests of the universe, to the interests of that great society of all sensible and intelligent beings, of which God himself is the immediate administrator and director."[6]

[5]*Wealth of Nations,* Book IV, ch. 7.
[6]*Ibid.,* Book V, ch. i, part 3.

It must be noted that in Smith's conception the "wider interest" does not stop at the boundary of the national state. His was a real universalism in intent. *Laissez faire* was intended to establish a world community as well as a natural harmony of interests within each nation. Smith clearly belongs to the children of light. But the children of darkness were able to make good use of his creed. A dogma which was intended to guarantee the economic freedom of the individual became the "ideology" of vast corporate structures of a later period of capitalism, used by them, and still used, to prevent a proper political control of their power. His vision of international harmony was transmuted into the sorry realities of an international capitalism which recognized neither moral scruples nor political restraints in expanding its power over the world. His vision of a democratic harmony of society, founded upon the free play of economic forces, was refuted by the tragic realities of the class conflicts in western society. Individual and collective egotism usually employed the political philosophy of this creed, but always defied the moral idealism which informed it.

The political theory of liberalism, as distinct from the economic theory, based its confidence in the identity of particular and universal interests, not so much upon the natural limits of egotism as upon either the capacity of reason to transmute egotism into a concern for the general welfare, or upon the ability of government to overcome the potential conflict of wills in society. But even when this confidence lies in reason or in government, the actual character of the egotism which must be restrained is frequently measured in the dimension of the natural impulse of survival only. Thus John Locke, who thinks government necessary in order to overcome the "inconvenience of the state of nature," sees self-interest in conflict with the general interest only on the low level where "self-preservation" stands in contrast to the interests of others. He therefore can express the sense of obligation to others in terms which assume no final conflict between egotism and the wider interest: "Everyone," he writes, "as he is bound to preserve himself and not to quit his station willfully, so by the like reason, when his own preservation comes not into competition, ought as much as he can preserve the rest of mankind."[7] This is obviously no creed of a moral cynic; but neither is it a profound expression of the sense of universal obligation. For most

[7]John Locke, *Two Treatises on Government*, Book II, ch. 2, par. 6.

of the gigantic conflicts of will in human history,
whether between individuals or groups, take place
on a level, where "self-preservation" is not immediately but only indirectly involved. They are
conflicts of rival lusts and ambitions.

The general confidence of an identity between
self-interest and the commonweal, which underlies
liberal democratic political theory, is succinctly
expressed in Thomas Paine's simple creed: "Public
good is not a term opposed to the good of the individual; on the contrary it is the good of every
individual collected. It is the good of all, because
it is the good of every one; for as the public body
is every individual collected, so the public good is
the collected good of those individuals."[8]

While there is a sense in which this identity between a particular and the general interest is ultimately true, it is never absolutely true in an immediate situation; and such identity as could be
validly claimed in an immediate situation is not
usually recognized by the proponents of particular
interest.[9] Human intelligence is never as pure an

---

[8]*Dissertations on Government, The Affairs of the Bank, and
Paper-Money* (1786).

[9]The peril of inflation which faces nations in war-time is
a case in point. Each group seeks to secure a larger income,
and if all groups succeeded, the gap between increased income
and limited consumer goods available to satisfy consumer de-

instrument of the universal perspective as the liberal democratic theory assumes, though neither is it as purely the instrument of the ego, as is assumed by the anti-democratic theory, derived from the pessimism of such men as Thomas Hobbes and Martin Luther.

The most naïve form of the democratic faith in an identity between the individual and the general interest is developed by the utilitarians of the eighteenth and nineteenth centuries. Their theory manages to extract a covertly expressed sense of obligation toward the "greatest good of the greatest number" from a hedonistic analysis of morals which really lacks all logical presuppositions for any idea of obligation, and which cannot logically rise above an egoistic view of life. This utilitarianism therefore expresses the stupidity of the children of light in its most vivid form. Traditional moralists may

---

mand would be widened to the point at which all groups would suffer from higher prices. But this does not deter short-sighted groups from seeking special advantages which threaten the commonweal. Nor would such special advantage threaten the welfare of the whole, if it could be confined to a single group which desires the advantage. The problem is further complicated by the fact that an inflationary peril never develops in a "just" social situation. Some groups therefore have a moral right to demand that their share of the common social fund be increased before the total situation is "frozen." But who is to determine just how much "injustice" can be redressed by a better distribution of the common fund in war-time, before the procedure threatens the whole community?

point to any hedonistic doctrine as the creed of the
children of darkness, because it has no real escape
from egotism. But since it thinks it has, it illustrates
the stupidity of the children of light, rather than
the malice of the children of darkness. It must be
observed of course that the children of darkness
are well able to make use of such a creed. Utilitarianism's conception of the wise egotist, who in
his prudence manages to serve interests wider than
his own, supported exactly the same kind of political philosophy as Adam Smith's conception of
the harmless egotist, who did not even have to be
wise, since the providential laws of nature held his
egotism in check. So Jeremy Bentham's influence
was added to that of Adam Smith in support of
a *laissez-faire* political philosophy; and this philosophy encouraged an unrestrained expression of
human greed at the precise moment in history
when an advancing industrialism required more,
rather than less, moral and political restraint upon
economic forces.

It must be added that, whenever the democratic
idealists were challenged to explain the contrast
between the actual behaviour of men and their
conception of it, they had recourse to the evolu-
tionary hope; and declared with William Godwin,

that human history is moving toward a form of rationality which will finally achieve a perfect identity of self-interest and the public good.[10]

Perhaps the most remarkable proof of the power of this optimistic creed, which underlies democratic thought, is that Marxism, which is ostensibly a revolt against it, manages to express the same optimism in another form. While liberal democrats dreamed of a simple social harmony, to be achieved by a cool prudence and a calculating egotism, the actual facts of social history revealed that the static class struggle of agrarian societies had been fanned into the flames of a dynamic struggle. Marxism was the social creed and the social cry of those classes who knew by their miseries that the creed of the liberal optimists was a snare and a delusion. Marxism insisted that the increasingly overt social conflict in democratic society would have to become even more overt, and would finally be fought to a bitter conclusion. But Marxism was also convinced that after the triumph of the lower classes of society, a new society would emerge in which exactly that kind of harmony between all social forces would be established, which Adam Smith had regarded as a possibility for any kind of so-

---

[10]William Godwin, *Political Justice,* Book VIII, ch. ix.

ciety. The similarities between classical *laissez-faire* theory and the vision of an anarchistic millennium in Marxism are significant, whatever may be the superficial differences. Thus the provisionally cynical Lenin, who can trace all the complexities of social conflict in contemporary society with penetrating shrewdness, can also express the utopian hope that the revolution will usher in a period of history which will culminate in the Marxist millennium of anarchism. "All need for force will vanish," declared Lenin, "since people will grow accustomed to observing the elementary conditions of social existence without force and without subjection."[11]

The Roman Catholic polemic against Marxism is no more valid than its strictures against democratic liberalism. The charge that this is a creed of moral cynicism cannot be justified. However strong the dose of provisional cynicism, which the creed may contain, it is a sentimental and not a cynical creed. The Marxists, too, are children of light. Their provisional cynicism does not even save them from the usual stupidity, nor from the fate, of other stupid children of light. That fate is to have their creed become the vehicle and instru-

[11]Lenin, *Toward the Seizure of Power,* Vol. II, p. 214.

ment of the children of darkness. A new oligarchy is arising in Russia, the spiritual characteristics of which can hardly be distinguished from those of the American "go-getters" of the latter nineteenth and early twentieth centuries. And in the light of history Stalin will probably have the same relation to the early dreamers of the Marxist dreams which Napoleon has to the liberal dreamers of the eighteenth century.

IV

Democratic theory, whether in its liberal or in its more radical form, is just as stupid in analyzing the relation between the national and the international community as in seeking a too simple harmony between the individual and the national community. Here, too, modern liberal culture exhibits few traces of moral cynicism. The morally autonomous modern national state does indeed arise; and it acknowledges no law beyond its interests. The actual behaviour of the nations is cynical. But the creed of liberal civilization is sentimental. This is true not only of the theorists whose creed was used by the architects of economic imperialism and of the more covert forms of national egotism in the international community, but also of those whose theories were appropriated by the proponents of an explicit national egotism. A straight line runs from Mazzini to Mussolini in the history of Italian nationalism. Yet there was not a touch of moral cynicism in the thought of Mazzini. He was, on the contrary, a pure universalist.[12]

Even the philosophy of German romanticism, which has been accused with some justification of making specific contributions to the creed of German Nazism, reveals the stupidity of the children of light much more than the malice of the children of darkness. There is of course a strong note of moral nihilism in the final fruit of this romantic movement as we have it in Nietzsche; though even Nietzsche was no nationalist. But the earlier romantics usually express the same combination of

---

[12]"Your first duty," wrote Mazzini, "first as regards importance, is toward humanity. You are men before you are citizens and fathers. If you do not embrace the whole human family in your affections, if you do not bear witness to the unity of that family, if—you are not ready, if able, to aid the unhappy,—you violate your law of life and you comprehend not that religion which will be the guide and blessing of the future."

Mazzini held kings responsible for national egotism: "The first priests of the fatal worship [of self-interest] were the kings, princes and evil governments. They invented the horrible formula: every one for himself. They knew that they would thus create egoism and that between the egoist and the slave there is but one step." *The Duties of Man,* ch. xii.

individualism and universalism which character-
izes the theory of the more naturalistic and ration-
alistic democrats of the western countries. Fichte
resolved the conflict between the individual and
the community through the instrumentality of the
"just law" almost as easily as the utilitarians resolved it by the calculations of the prudent egotist
and as easily as Rousseau resolved it by his conception of a "general will," which would fulfill the
best purposes of each individual will. This was no
creed of a community, making itself the idolatrous
end of human existence. The theory was actually
truer than the more individualistic and naturalistic
forms of the democratic creed; for romanticism
understood that the individual requires the community for his fulfillment. Thus even Hegel, who
is sometimes regarded as the father of state absolutism in modern culture, thought of the national
state as providing "for the reasonable will, insofar
as it is in the individual only implicitly the universal will coming to a consciousness and an understanding of itself and being found."[13]

This was not the creed of a collective egotism
which negated the right of the individual. Rather
it was a theory which, unlike the more purely dem-

[13]*Philosophy of Mind,* Sect. II, par. 539.

ocratic creed, understood the necessity of social fulfilment for the individual, and which, in common with the more liberal theories, regarded this as a much too simple process.

If the theory was not directed toward the annihilation of the individual, as is the creed of modern religious nationalism, to what degree was it directed against the universal community? Was it an expression of the national community's defiance of any interest or law above and beyond itself? This also is not the case. Herder believed that "fatherlands" might "lie peaceably side by side and aid each other as families. It is the grossest barbarity of human speech to speak of fatherlands in bloody battle with each other." Unfortunately this is something more than a barbarity of speech. Herder was a universalist, who thought a nice harmony between various communities could be achieved if only the right would be granted to each to express itself according to its unique and peculiar genius. He thought the false universalism of imperialism, according to which one community makes itself the standard and the governor of others, was merely the consequence of a false philosophy, whereas it is in fact one of the perennial corruptions of man's collective life.

Fichte, too, was a universalist who was fully conscious of moral obligations which transcend the national community. His difficulty, like that of all the children of light, was that he had a too easy resolution of the conflict between the nation and the community of nations. He thought that philosophy, particularly German philosophy, could achieve a synthesis between national and universal interest. "The patriot," he declared, "wishes the purpose of mankind to be reached first of all in that nation of which he is a member. . . . This purpose is the only possible patriotic goal. . . . Cosmopolitanism is the will that the purpose of life and of man be attained in all mankind, Patriotism is the will that this purpose be attained first of all in that nation of which we are members."[14] It is absurd to regard such doctrine as the dogma of national egotism, though Fichte could not express it without insinuating a certain degree of national pride into it. The pride took the form of the complacent assumption that German philosophy enabled the German nation to achieve a more perfect relation to the community of mankind than any other nation. He was, in other words,

---

[14]"Patriotische Dialoge," in *Nachgelassene Werker,* Vol. III, p. 226.

one of the many stupid children of light, who failed to understand the difficulty of the problem which he was considering; and his blindness included failure to see the significance of the implicit denial of an ideal in the thought and action of the very idealist who propounds it.

Hegel, too, belongs to the children of light. To be sure he saw little possibility of constructing a legal structure of universal proportions which might guard the interests of the universal community and place a check upon the will of nations. He declared "states find themselves in a natural, more than a legal, relation to each other. Therefore there is a continuous struggle between them. . . . They maintain and procure their rights through their own power and must as a matter of necessity plunge into war."[15] It may be observed in passing that this is a more accurate description of the actual realities of international relations than that of any of the theorists thus far considered. But the question is whether Hegel regarded this actual situation as morally normative. Hegel's thought upon this matter was ambiguous. On the one hand he tended to regard the demands of the state as final because he saw no way of achieving a legal or political im-

---

[15]*Saemmtliche Werker,* Vol. III, p. 74.

plementation of the inchoate community which
lies beyond the state. But on the other hand he
believed that a more ultimate law stood over the
nation, that it "had its real content in *Weltgeschichte,* the realm of the world mind which
holds the supreme absolute truth."[16] This mind, he
believed, "constitutes itself the absolute judge over
states." The nation is thus politically, but not morally, autonomous. This is no doctrine of moral cynicism. Rather it is a sentimental doctrine. Hegel
imagined that the nation, free of political but not
of moral inhibitions, could nevertheless, by thinking "in Weltgeschichte" (that is, by becoming fully
conscious of its relation to mankind), thereby "lay
hold of its concrete universality."[17] The error is
very similar to that of Fichte and of all the universalists, whether naturalistic or idealistic, posi-
tivist or romantic. It is the error of a too great re-
liance upon the human capacity for transcendence
over self-interest. There is indeed such a capacity.
If there were not, any form of social harmony
among men would be impossible; and certainly a
democratic version of such harmony would be
quite unthinkable. But the same man who displays

---

[16]*Philosophy of Right,* par. 33.
[17]*Philosophy of Mind,* Sect. II, par. 552.

this capacity also reveals varying degrees of the power of self-interest and of the subservience of the mind to these interests. Sometimes this egotism stands in frank contradiction to the professed ideal or sense of obligation to higher and wider values; and sometimes it uses the ideal as its instrument.

It is this fact which a few pessimists in our modern culture have realized, only to draw undemocratic and sometimes completely cynical conclusions from it. The democratic idealists of practically all schools of thought have managed to remain remarkably oblivious to the obvious facts. Democratic theory therefore has not squared with the facts of history. This grave defect in democratic theory was comparatively innocuous in the heyday of the bourgeois period, when the youth and the power of democratic civilization surmounted all errors of judgment and confusions of mind. But in this latter day, when it has become important to save what is valuable in democratic life from the destruction of what is false in bourgeois civilization, it has also become necessary to distinguish what is false in democratic theory from what is true in democratic life.

The preservation of a democratic civilization requires the wisdom of the serpent and the harmlessness of the dove. The children of light must be armed with the wisdom of the children of darkness but remain free from their malice. They must know the power of self-interest in human society without giving it moral justification. They must have this wisdom in order that they may beguile, deflect, harness and restrain self-interest, individual and collective, for the sake of the community.

CHAPTER TWO

THE INDIVIDUAL AND THE COMMUNITY

I

BOURGEOIS DEMOCRACY, as we now have it, was established primarily to give the individual freedom from the traditional cultural, social and political restraints of the feudal-medieval world. The democratic idealists of the eighteenth century did not anticipate any significant tension between the individual and the community, because they failed to gauge the indeterminate vitalities and ambitions which may arise from any center of life, whether individual or social. They did not fear the peril of anarchy which might arise from individual ambitions, because they estimated the forces of human nature in terms of man's relation to "nature" or to "reason" and thought that there were adequate checks upon inordinate ambition in either

42

one or the other. They believed, in short, that men were essentially tame, cool and calculating and that individual egotism did not rise beyond the limits of nature's impulse of self-preservation.

They did not fear the power, ambition or collective egotism of the community because they associated undue political restraints upon the individual with the particular form of such restraints which they had known in a feudal economic order on a monarchical political order. They thought they had reduced the power of the community to minimal proportions by the constitutional principles of democratic government, according to which government had only negative powers and was limited to the adjudication of disputes or to the rôle of a traffic policeman, maintaining minimal order.

There were of course modern realists and pessimists who understood the dynamic character of human life, and knew that human ambitions may easily become inordinate and thereby imperil the peace of the community. These pessimists fashioned anti-democratic political theories, believing that only a strong government and one which stood above the rivalries and competitions which it would have to suppress would be able to maintain the peace of the community. Unfortunately these pessimists were betrayed into two errors which have proved as grievous as the illusions of the optimists. They assigned only the negative task of suppression to government; and they failed to provide for any checks upon the inordinate ambitions which the community as such, or its rulers, might conceive and thereby imperil the rights and interests of the individual.

The first error was due to their too consistent pessimism. In the case of both Luther and Thomas Hobbes (the one of whom elaborated a religious and the other a secular version of a purely pessimistic analysis of man's nature) human desires are regarded as inherently inordinate, and human character is believed to be practically devoid of inner checks upon expansive desires. In their opinion the business of government is to maintain order by repression. Though it is true that government must have the power to subdue recalcitrance, it also has a more positive function. It must guide, direct, deflect and rechannel conflicting and competing forces in a community in the interest of a higher order. It must provide instruments for the expression of the individual's sense of obligation to the community as well as weapons against the individual's anti-social lusts and ambitions.

The second error reveals the moral naïveté of every form of absolutistic political theory. It identifies the national community with the universal and fails to recognize that the nation is also an egocentric force in history, tempted on the one hand to claim a too unconditioned position in relation to the individuals and to the subordinate institutions in the national community; and on the other hand to become a source of anarchy in the larger community of nations. Furthermore it identifies the interests of the ruler or the ruling oligarchy of a community too simply with the interests of the community. Therefore it fails to provide checks against the inordinate impulses to power, to which all rulers are tempted.[1] This latter error may be made by some optimists as well as pessimists. The political theory of Rousseau contains the conception of a "general will" which is supposedly the final harmony of conflicting individual wills. This conception obscures the fact that there is a conflict of wills in every living community, and that the victorious will is at least partly fashioned and

---

[1] Thomas Hobbes identifies the interests of the ruler with those of the community in the following implausible words: "In monarchy the private interest is the same with the public interest because no prince can be rich and glorious nor secure, whose subjects are poor or weak or contemptible." *Leviathan*, ch. 19.

crystallized by the ruling oligarchy which has the instruments to express it. In a democratic society there is presumably some concurrence between the will of the rulers and that of the majority; but the Rousseauistic conception leads to constitutional forms which offer inadequate safeguards to the minority.

Marxist social theory betrays striking similarities to Rousseau's conceptions. It fails to anticipate the rise of a ruling group in a socialist society. When the group does arise, the theories are forced to obscure the initiative of the rulers, and to pretend that the policies at which the leaders arrive represent merely the expression of what the multitude has conceived.[2]

Democracy cannot be validated purely upon the basis of early democratic theory. Some of the facts of human nature, discerned by Hobbes and Luther, must be taken into consideration. These facts prove a democratic society to be more difficult of achievement than idealistic democratic theory assumes; but they also prove it to be more necessary. For certainly one perennial justification for democracy is that it arms the individual with political and

---

[2]Sidney and Beatrice Webb's description of the Soviet five-year plan betrays this naïve illusion. *Cf. Soviet Communism: A New Civilisation,* Vol. II, ch. viii.

constitutional power to resist the inordinate ambition of rulers, and to check the tendency of the
community to achieve order at the price of liberty.

II

While democratic theorists failed to measure the
full dimensions and the dynamic quality of human
vitalities, the undemocratic constitutionalists saw
the destructive but not the creative possibilities of
individual vitality and ambition and appreciated
the necessity, but not the peril, of strong government. Preoccupation with the perils of collective
forms of ambition produce social theories which
emphasize freedom at the expense of order, ending
finally in the philosophy of anarchism. Preoccupation with the perils of individual inordinateness, on
the other hand, allows the fear of anarchy to bear
the fruit of connivance with tyranny.

Actually human vitalities express themselves
from both individual and collective centers in many
directions, and both are capable of unpredictable
creative and destructive consequences. Nor can the
line between the creative and the inordinate be
simply drawn. Were the priestly and military or-

ganizers of the early Egyptian and Babylonian empires creative or destructive? They created new and vaster communities but also finally destroyed them by the very power through which they had created them.

The indeterminate character of human vitalities, including their most spiritualized forms, must be considered in its various dimensions if the problem of democratic unity is to be fully understood. Three aspects must be considered particularly. (1) The individual is related to the community (in its various levels and extensions) in such a way that the highest reaches of his individuality are dependent upon the social substance out of which they arise and they must find their end and fulfillment in the community. No simple limit can be placed upon the degree of intimacy to the community, and the breadth and extent of community which the individual requires for his life.

(2) Both individual and collective centers of human vitality may be endlessly elaborated. Any premature definition of what the limits of these elaborations ought to be inevitably destroys and suppresses legitimate forms of life and culture. But this capacity for human creativity also involves the destructive capacity of human vitality. Vitalities

may be developed inordinately. Various forms of vitality may come in conflict with one another, or one form may illegitimately suppress another. The tension between the various forms may threaten or destroy the harmony and peace of the community. The indeterminate creativity of history validates the idea of a free or democratic society, which refuses to place premature checks upon human vitalities. The destructive possibilities of these vitalities prove democracy to be a more difficult achievement than is usually supposed.

(3) Individual vitality rises in indeterminate degree over all social and communal concretions of life. The freedom of the human spirit over the natural process makes history possible. The transcendent perspective of the individual over the historical process makes history perpetually creative and capable of producing new forms; but it also means that the individual finally has some vantage point over history itself. Man is able to ask some questions about the meaning of life, for which the course of history cannot supply adequate answers; and to seek after fulfillments of meaning for which there are no satisfactions in the moral ambiguities of history. This fact negates the "secularism" of modern democratic idealism and refutes the erro·

neous belief that man would be more creative in society and history if he would confine himself within its limits. The three forms of indeterminate possibilities must be studied more fully in order.

III

The individual and the community are related to each other on many levels. The highest reaches of individual consciousness and awareness are rooted in social experience and find their ultimate meaning in relation to the community. The individual is the product of the whole socio-historical process, though he may reach a height of uniqueness which seems to transcend his social history completely. His individual decisions and achievements grow into, as well as out of, the community and find their final meaning in the community. Even the highest forms of art avail themselves of tools and forms, of characteristic insights and styles which betray the time and place of the artist; and if they rise to very great heights of individual insight they will also achieve a corresponding height of universal validity. They will illustrate, or penetrate into, some universal, rather than some particular and dated experience, and thereby will illumine the life of a more timeless and wider community. Thus Shakespeare is the product of Elizabethan England, and Cervantes springs from the soil of a dying Spanish feudalism, but each in his uniqueness rises to a universal perspective which makes the ages, and all civilized communities, his debtors.

The individualism of bourgeois democracy, in which the social substance of human existence was misunderstood in thought, and reduced to minimal proportions in practice, was partly derived from illusions which seemed plausible enough in the early stages of the bourgeois rebellion against feudalism. The new commercial civilization offered individuals a wider variety of vocational choices than the old agrarian community. The competence of the craftsman and the skill of the trader gave men a new and more flexible form of social power, while industrial and commercial wealth was more mobile and dynamic than the old wealth of land ownership. The new urban communities created conditions of anonymity in which the more organic ties to family and clan, which disciplined life in the rural community, were broken; and the urban man celebrated his independence of the older social restraints, which had both formed and limited his life. History really seemed to be in the mastery of the individual. The range of his choices was wider; and his position in society seemed to be the consequence of his own initiative, rather than some hereditary influence.

Even man's dependence upon nature appeared to be broken in the city. The rhythms of seedtime and harvest, of waxing and waning moon, were very remote from the perspective of urban man. Therefore the man of the soil's religious reverence and awe before the forces of nature beyond his control, and his sense of gratitude for nature's beneficence (celebrated in all ages in harvest festivals) atrophied in urban life.

Thus the sense of bourgeois self-sufficiency was created. Human freedom had increased; but not to the degree imagined in liberal democratic thought. A particularly pathetic aspect of this ideal of individual self-sufficiency is given by the fact that early bourgeois culture was the childhood of a technical civilization in which men would become intimately related to, and dependent upon, vaster and vaster historical forces. This culture culminated in a period in which Frenchmen who wanted to know nothing about Danzig and Englishmen, who wanted to know nothing about Czecho-Slovakia, were drawn into universal wars which had their beginnings in these very areas.

The bourgeois sense of individual mastery over historical destiny and the liberal idea of a self-sufficient individual is admirably expressed in the "social contract" theory of the origin of civil government. The theory is ostensibly a justification of democratic government (though Hobbes used it to justify the creation of despotic government through the individual's abnegation of his freedom in favor of the community's authority). But in reality the theory was more than a concept of the origin and nature of government. It assumes that communities, and not merely governments, are created by a fiat of the human will. It also perpetuates the illusion that communities remain primarily the instruments of atomic individuals, who are forced to create some kind of minimal order for their common life, presumably because the presence of many other such individuals in some limited area, makes "traffic rules" necessary.

The theory completely obscures the primordial character of the human community and the power of historical destiny over human decisions. Every human decision about the character of a community or its government has always been taken in the light of, and been limited by, the actualities of the community which existed before the decision was taken. There is freedom in history; otherwise tribal communities, held together by consanguinity and gregariousness, would not have developed into the wider communities of empires and nations, in which human intelligence has added various artifacts to nature's original minimal force of social cohesion. But there is no absolute freedom in history; for every choice is limited by the stuff which nature and previous history present to the hour of decision. Even today when statesmen deal with global politics they must consider ethnic and geographic facts which represent nature's limitations upon man's decisions; and they must take account of affinities and animosities which ages of previous history have created.

A significant refutation of bourgeois individualism lies in the fact that the more the individual ostensibly emerges from the community to establish his own independence and uniqueness, the more he becomes dependent upon a wider system of mutual services. Men have never been individually self-sufficient; but older pastoral and agrarian societies had smaller units of self-sufficiency than are possible today. Every specialization of unique gifts in the life of the individual, every elaboration of special skills means that a larger community is required to support the individual. It also means that instruments and skills are created which can bind a larger community together in one unit of cooperation, though it must be admitted that the political skills, which order the life of the larger community, always lag behind the technical skills which create the potential society in which a greater order is required.

The individual's dependence upon the community for the foundation upon which the pinnacle of his uniqueness stands, and the stuff out of which particular and special forms of his vitality are created is matched by his need of the community as the partial end, justification and fulfillment of his existence. The ideal of individual self-sufficiency, so exalted in our liberal culture, is recognized in Christian thought as one form of the primal sin. For self-love, which is the root of all sin, takes two social forms. One of them is the domination of other life by the self. The second is the sin of isolationism. The self can be its true self only by continued transcendence over self. This self-transcendence either ends in mystic otherworldliness or it must be transmuted into indeterminate realizations of the self in the life of others. By the responsibilities which men have to their family and community and to many common enterprises, they are drawn out of themselves to become their true selves. The indeterminate character of human freedom makes it impossible to set any limits of intensity or extent to this social responsibility. (We have spoken of the community thus far without defining its boundaries. Family and nation have become the inner and outer confines of the community for most men; but we have advisedly left the limits undefined because we must presently consider the fact that no bounds can be finally placed upon man's responsibility to his fellows or upon his need of their help.)

It is significant that the mood which prompted the social-contract theory of government finally also generated a similar theory of family life in the heydey of bourgeois culture. The theory assumed that two people could establish a sexual partnership by a revocable contract and that the contract should preserve as much liberty as possible for each partner. But a healthy marriage produces children who are not revocable. It initiates an organic process of mutuality which outruns any decision which created it. This is not to say that all marriages should be indissoluble or should be legally maintained when they have been broken in fact; but the organic character of social relationships certainly refutes the modern conception of the free individual who must preserve his freedom even in the most organic forms of togetherness, and must be intent upon the perpetual possibility of reclaiming the absolute freedom which was "compromised" in the marriage relationship.

Marxist collectivism was, on the whole, a healthy and inevitable revolt against bourgeois individualism. The new class of industrial workers had found the limits of individual uniqueness and freedom in the intensive togetherness of the modern industrial plant. They knew themselves to be members, one of another. They also sensed their true relation to the vast forces of historical destiny, which human decisions may affect and deflect but not negate. Their sense of the relation of decision to destiny was sometimes corrupted by the mechanistic conceptions of life and history, which urban man, whether bourgeois or proletarian, tends to conceive. Marxists therefore spoke of the "laws of motion" in society, and tried to comprehend the dynamics of society as if they were problems in social physics. But at best Marxism preserved a proper dialectical balance between destiny and decision in history, while it refuted the illusions of individual self-sufficiency.

Marxism is sometimes counted among the children of darkness, the barbarians, who have snuffed out the individual in the demonic glorification of the collective. It must be observed, however, that if the difference in practice between national collectivists and Marxists is not always very great, the difference in theory is immense. The similarity in practice arises from the fact that a dictatorship, which according to the theory is to be only provisional, becomes permanent. The difference in theory is that Marxism really desires a perfect harmony between the individual and the community. "One must always avoid," declares Marx, "setting up 'society' as an abstraction, opposed to the individual. The individual is the social entity. The expression of his life is therefore an expression and verification of the life of society."[3]

In this vision Marxism rightly conceives the social character of all individual existence. But its dream of a frictionless harmony and identity between individual and community is an illusion. The

[3]*Oekonomische-philosophische Manuskripte,* p. 117.

error is partly the consequence of the Marxist belief that the tendency toward domination is caused
by the class structure of human society and will
disappear with the revolution which destroys the
class system. The materialist conception of human
consciousness in Marxist theory obscures both the
creative and destructive transcendence of individual consciousness over any and every social and
historical concretion of life. Life requires a more
organic and mutual form than bourgeois democratic theory provides for it; but the social substance of life is richer and more various, and has
greater depths and tensions than are envisaged in
the Marxist dream of social harmony.

IV

The deficiency of both bourgeois and Marxist
social theory in estimating the indeterminate possibilities of historic vitalities, as they express themselves in both individual and collective terms, is
derived from their common effort to understand
man without considering the final dimension of his
spirit: his transcendent freedom over both the natural and the historical process in which he is involved. This freedom accounts for both the crea-

tive and destructive possibilities in human history.
The difference between bourgeois liberalism and
Marxism leads the former to regard the world of
competitive economic life as essentially tame or
capable of being tamed; while the latter sees all
the demonic fury of this struggle, and anticipates
its final debacle. But Marxism expects men to be as
tame and social on the other side of the revolution
as Adam Smith and Jeremy Bentham thought them
to be tame and prudential on this side of the revolution. The difference between the two theories
therefore prompts contradictory estimates of particular social situations; but the similarity between
them results in identical estimates of the ultimate
human and historical situation. The social harmony of which Marxism dreams would eliminate
the destructive power of human freedom; but it
would also destroy the creative possibilities of human life. The Marxist theory, when applied to a
particular situation—as for instance to that curious
"Earnest" of the ideal society, Russia—leads to as
many miscalculations of the actual dynamic forces
at work in such a society as does liberal theory,
when it deals with contemporary capitalistic society.

The expansive character of human ambitions,

lusts, fears and desires is the consequence of the indeterminate transcendence of man's spirit over the physical, natural and historical processes in which he is involved. Every human desire and vitality has a core of natural need and no spiritual transmutation ever eliminates this natural core. The hunger, sex and survival impulses lie at the foundation of human vitality; but they are endlessly elaborated. This is why psychology can never be absolutely precise, without being arbitrary, in defining even natural "instincts" or "prepotent reflexes." The sex impulse is never purely as biological in man as in the brute. It is creatively related to the artistic impulse and lies at the foundation of the family organization, which in turn is the nucleus of larger organizations of the human community. But sex can also become the perverse obsession of man because he has the freedom to center his life inordinately in one impulse, while the economy of nature preserves a pre-established harmony of the various vitalities.

Economic desires are never merely the expression of the hunger or the survival impulse in human life. The desires for "power and glory" are subtly compounded with the more primeval impulse. The lion's desire for food is satisfied when his maw is crammed. Man's desire for food is more easily limited than other human desires; yet the hunger impulse is subject to the endless refinements and perversions of the gourmand. Shelter and raiment have much more extensible limits than food. Man's coat is never merely a cloak for his nakedness but the badge of his vocation, or the expression of an artistic impulse, or a method of attracting the other sex, or a proof of social position. Man's house is not merely his shelter but, even more than his raiment, the expression of his personality and the symbol of his power, position and prestige. The houses and the raiment of the poor remain closer to the original "natural" requirement; but it is significant that the power to transmute them into something more spiritual and symbolic is invariably exploited.

The economic activities by which these desires are satisfied are subject to an even greater transmutation than the desires themselves. Every skill, or every organization of skill, in industry or trade, is a form of social power. Every such social power seeks to enhance or to stabilize itself by the acquisition of property. If economic power becomes great enough, it seeks to transmute itself into political power. Whenever a power, which is generated in specific functions, becomes strong enough to make the step possible or plausible, it seeks to participate in organizing the community. Thus the societies of the past have been organized by various types of oligarchies who had the most significant or most dominant social power of their epoch. Early societies were organized and dominated by priests and warriors, either in competition or in cooperation with each other, while in the modern period the commercial and industrial oligarchy has sought to gain added political hegemony in the bourgeois community. The satisfaction of primary needs, particularly if it is achieved with a fair degree of equity, may ease social friction. Contrariwise a threatened famine, or any threat to the satisfaction of elementary needs, may accentuate conflict and reduce the social struggle to its elemental proportions. But there is no basis for the Marxist hope that an "economy of abundance" will guarantee social peace; for men may fight as desperately for "power and glory" as for bread.

A free society is justified by the fact that the indeterminate possibilities of human vitality may be creative. Every definition of the restraints which must be placed upon these vitalities must be tentative; because all such definitions, which are themselves the products of specific historical insights, may prematurely arrest or suppress a legitimate vitality, if they are made absolute and fixed. The community must constantly re-examine the presuppositions upon which it orders its life, because no age can fully anticipate or predict the legitimate and creative vitalities which may arise in subsequent ages.

The limitations upon freedom in a society are justified, on the other hand, by the fact that the vitalities may be destructive. We have already noted that the justification of classical *laissez-faire* theories was the mistaken belief that human passions were naturally ordinate and limited. It must be added that there are also some types of social theory, which understand the boundless character of man's vitalities and yet advocate unlimited freedom. In the nineteenth century Darwinian, rather than physiocratic, presuppositions frequently furnished the *rationale* of *laissez-faire* social theory.[4] The physiocrats trusted the pre-established harmony of nature. The Darwinians attributed a moral historical significance to the struggles of nature.

---

[4] A typical American exponent of the idea that the human community must allow a free play of social competition in the hope of the survival of the best was William Graham Sumner. *Cf.: What Social Classes Owe to Each Other.*

They failed to understand that human society is a vast moral and historical artifact, which would be destroyed if natural conflicts and contests between various vitalities were not mitigated, managed and arbitrated. Both the intensity and the breadth of social cohesion have been historically created. A conflict against the background of this historical cohesion is never, as in the natural world, a limited conflict between two simple or individual units of vitality. A contest between monopolistic and smaller units of economic power, for instance, is not a "natural" contest. The unequal power of one contestant is the product of the tendency toward centralization of power in the processes of a technical civilization. The power is a social and historical accretion; and the community must decide whether it is in the interest of justice to reduce monopolistic control artificially for the sake of reestablishing the old pattern of "fair competition," or whether it is wiser to allow the process of centralization of economic power to continue until the monopolistic centers have destroyed all competition. But, if the second alternative is chosen, the community faces the new problem of bringing the centralized economic power under communal control. These historical contests of power must be managed, supervised, and suppressed by the community, precisely because they do not move within the limits of "nature." The battleground is the human community and not the animal herd; and the contestants are armed with powers which have been drawn from the historical and communal process.

Modern libertarian doctrines, all of which implicitly or explicitly look forward to an anarchistic culmination of the historical process, are not limited to those theories which reduce the community to the dimensions of nature and which regard either the conflicts or the harmonies of nature as normative. Many of them place their trust in a developing reason, as the force which will progressively eliminate social tension and conflict and obviate the use of coercion in maintaining order. Reason is provisionally an organ of the universal, as against the particular, interest; and growing rationality has thus undoubtedly contributed to the extension of human communities. Even practical reason has contributed to this end; for it has furnished the technical and political instruments which bind larger communities together in one unit of mutual dependence.

Yet there is no evidence that reason is becoming progressively disembodied. It always remains organically related to a particular center of vitality, individual and collective; and it is therefore always a weapon of defense and attack for this vitality against competing vitalities, as well as a transcendent force which arbitrates between conflicting vitalities. A high perspective of reason may as easily enlarge the realm of dominion of an imperial self as mitigate expansive desires in the interest of the harmony of the whole. No community, whether national or international, can maintain its order if it cannot finally limit expansive impulses by coercion.

But the question arises, how the strategies of coercion of the community are judged and prevented from becoming inordinate. If it is granted that both the rulers and the community as such are also centers of vitality and expansive impulse, would not their use of restrictive power be purely arbitrary if it were not informed by some general principles of justice, which define the right order of life in a community? The fact is that there are no living communities which do not have some notions of justice, beyond their historic laws, by which they seek to gauge the justice of their legislative enactments. Such general principles are known as natural law in both Catholic and earlier liberal thought. Even when, as in the present stage of liberal democratic thought, moral theory has become too relativistic to make appeal to natural law as plausible as in other centuries, every human society does have something like a natural-law concept; for it assumes that there are more immutable and purer principles .of justice than those actually embodied in its obviously relative laws.

The final question to confront the proponent of a democratic and free society is whether the freedom of a society should extend to the point of allowing these principles to be called into question. Should they not stand above criticism or amendment? If they are themselves subjected to the democratic process and if they are made dependent upon the moods and vagaries of various communities and epochs, have we not sacrificed the final criterion of justice and order, by which we might set bounds to what is inordinate in both individual and collective impulses?

It is on this question that Catholic Christianity has its final difficulties with the presuppositions of a democratic society in the modern, liberal sense, fearing, in the words of a recent pronouncement of the American bishops, that questions of "right and wrong" may be subjected to the caprice of majority decisions. For Catholicism believes that the principles of natural law are fixed and immutable, a faith which the secular physiocrats of the eighteenth century shared.[5] It believes that the freedom of a democratic society must stop short of calling these principles of natural law in question.

The liberal democratic tradition of our era gave a different answer to this question. It did not have very plausible reasons for its answer; but history has provided better ones. The truth is that the bourgeois democratic theory held to the idea of absolute and unrestricted liberty, partly because it assumed the unlimited right of private judgment to be one of the "inalienable" rights which were guaranteed by the liberal version of the natural law.[6] Its adherence to the principle of complete liberty

---

[5]Catholic theory regards natural law as prescriptive and as derived from "right reason," whereas modern naturalism frequently defines it as merely descriptive, that is, as the law, which men may observe by analyzing the facts of nature. Jacques Maritain defines the natural law as "an order or a disposition which human reason can discover and according to which the human will must act in order to attune itself to the necessary ends of the human being." *The Rights of Man and Natural Law,* p. 61.

[6]The fact that the content of the natural law as Catholicism conceives it differs so widely from the content of the natural law as the eighteenth century conceived it, though the contents of both are supposed to represent "self-evident" truths of reason, must make the critical student sceptical.

of private judgment was also partly derived from its simple confidence in human reason. It was certain that reason would, when properly enlightened, affirm the "self-evident" truths of the natural law. Both the Catholic and the liberal confidence in the dictates of the natural law, thus rest upon a "non-existential" description of human reason. Both fail to appreciate the perennial corruptions of interest and passion which are introduced into any historical definition of even the most ideal and abstract moral principles. The Catholic confidence in the reason of common men was rightly less complete than that of the Enlightenment. Yet it wrongly sought to preserve some realm of institutional religious authority which would protect the uncorrupted truths of the natural law. The Enlightenment erroneously hoped for a general diffusion of intelligence which would make the truths of the natural law universally acceptable. Yet it rightly refused to reserve any area of authority which would not be subject to democratic criticism.

The reason this final democratic freedom is right, though the reasons given for it in the modern period are wrong, is that there is no historical reality, whether it be church or government, whether it be the reason of wise men or specialists, which is not involved in the flux and relativity of human existence; which is not subject to error and sin, and which is not tempted to exaggerate its errors and sins when they are made immune to criticism.

Every society needs working principles of justice, as criteria for its positive law and system of restraints. The profoundest of these actually transcend reason and lie rooted in religious conceptions of the meaning of existence. But every historical statement of them is subject to amendment. If it becomes fixed it will destroy some of the potentialities of a higher justice, which the mind of one generation is unable to anticipate in the life of subsequent eras.

Alfred Whitehead has distinguished between the "speculative" reason which "Plato shared with God" and the "pragmatic" reason which "Ulysses shared with the foxes."[7] The distinction is valid, provided it is understood that no sharp line can be drawn between the two. For man's spirit is a unity; and the most perfect vantage point of impartiality and disinterestedness in human reason remains in organic relation to a particular center of life, individual or collective, seeking to maintain its precarious existence against competing forms of

---

[7] *The Function of Reason,* pp. 23–30.

life and vitality. Even if a particular age should arrive at a "disinterested" vision of justice, in which individual interests and passions were completely transcended, it could not achieve a height of disinterestedness from which it could judge new emergents in history. It would use its apparatus of "self-evident truths" and "inalienable rights" as instruments of self-defence against the threat of the new vitality.

Because reason is something more than a weapon of self-interest it can be an instrument of justice; but since reason is never dissociated from the vitalities of life, individual and collective, it cannot be a pure instrument of the justice. Natural-law theories which derive absolutely valid principles of morals and politics from reason, invariably introduce contingent practical applications into the definition of the principle. This is particularly true when the natural law defines not merely moral but also political principles. It is easier to state a moral, than a political, principle in generally valid terms. Even hedonistic moral theory, which ostensibly has no other criterion of the good but pleasure, manages to introduce the criterion of the "greatest good of the greatest" number into its estimate of moral value, thereby proving that moral theory is practically unanimous in preferring the general to the particular interest, however variously the particular or the general interest may be defined. But political morality must be morally ambiguous because it cannot merely reject, but must also deflect, beguile, harness and use self-interest for the sake of a tolerable harmony of the whole.

The principles of political morality, being inherently more relative than those of pure morality, cannot be stated without the introduction of relative and contingent factors. In terms of pure moral principle one may contend that the ideal possibility of community is that every vital capacity should find its limit and its fulfillment in the harmony of the whole. In terms of political morality one must state the specific limits beyond which the individual cannot go if the minimal harmony of the community is to be preserved, and beyond which the community must not go if a decent minimal individual freedom is to be protected. But every precise definition of the requirements and the perils of government is historically conditioned by the comparative dangers of either a too strict order or of potential chaos in given periods of history.

Another example may be cited. Equality is a transcendent principle of justice and is therefore rightly regarded as one of the principles of natural law. But if a natural-law theory insists that absolute equality is a possibility of society, it becomes an ideology of some rebellious group which does not recognize that functional inequalities are necessary in all societies, however excessive they may be in the society which is under attack. If on the other hand functional inequalities are exactly defined the definitions are bound to contain dubious justifications of some functional privileges, possessed by the dominant classes of the culture which hazards the definition.

Even if natural-law concepts do not contain the ideological taint of a particular class or nation, they are bound to express the limited imagination of a particular epoch, which failed to take new historical possibilities into consideration. This alone would justify the ultimate freedom of a democratic society, in which not even the moral presuppositions upon which the society rests are withdrawn from constant scrutiny and re-examination. Only through such freedom can the premature arrest of new vitalities in history be prevented.

One might define a descending scale of relativity in the definition of moral and political principles. The moral principle may be more valid than the political principles which are derived from it. The political principles may have greater validity than the specific applications by which they are made relevant to a particular situation. And the specific applications may have a greater validity than the impulses and ambitions of the social hegemony of a given period which applies or pretends to apply them. But this descending scale of relativity never inhibits the bearers of power in a given period from claiming the sanctity of the pure principle for their power. There was a greater degree of validity in the ethical content of medieval natural law then in the social and political hegemony of priests and landed aristocrats in the feudal society. And there is more truth in the natural law as Jefferson conceived it, than there is justice in the social hegemony of monopolistic capitalism in our era, which maintains its prestige by appeals to Jefferson's principles. A society which exempts ultimate principles from criticisms will find difficulty in dealing with the historical forces which have appropriated these truths as their special possession.

Another and contrasting justification for a free society must be added. Sometimes new truth rides into history upon the back of an error. An authoritarian society would have prevented the new truth with the error. The idea that economic life is autonomous and ought not to be placed under either moral or political control is an error, for reasons which we have previously discussed. The self-regulating and self-balancing forces in economic life are not as strong as Adam Smith supposed. The propagation of this error has caused great damage in modern life. But a seed of truth was contained in the error. The intricacies of modern commerce and industry could not have developed if the medieval moral and political controls had been maintained; and even now when we know that all economic life must submit to moral discipline and political restraint, we must be careful to preserve whatever self-regulating forces exist in the economic process. If we do not, the task of control becomes too stupendous and the organs of control achieve proportions which endanger our liberty.

The truth in modern feminism came into history with some help from the errors of an inorganic and libertarian conception of the family and of an abstract rationalism which defied the facts of nature. The mother is biologically more intimately related to the child than the father. This fact limits the vocational freedom of women; for it makes moth-

erhood a more exclusive vocation than fatherhood,
which is indeed no more than an avocation. The
wider rights of women have been achieved in the
modern period, partly by defying this limitation
which nature places upon womanhood. But it is
also a fact that human personality rises in indeterminate freedom over biological function. The right
of women to explore and develop their capacities
beyond their family function, was unduly restricted
in all previous societies. It was finally acknowledged in our society, partly because the bourgeois
community had lost some of its appreciation of
the organic integrity of the family. Had this error
been prematurely suppressed, the new freedom of
women would have been suppressed also. It must
be added that the wisdom of the past which recognized the hazard to family life in the freedom of
women, was not devoid of the taint of male "ideology." The male oligarchy used fixed principles
of natural law to preserve its privileges and powers against a new emergent in history.

The freedom of society is thus made necessary
by the fact that human vitalities have no simply
definable limits.[8] The restraints which all human

[8]Jacques Maritain writes in his *The Rights of Man and
Natural Law:* "Natural law is the ensemble of things to do
and not to do which follow therefrom in a *necessary* fashion

communities place upon human impulses and ambitions are made necessary by the fact that all
man's vitalities tend to defy any defined limits. But
since the community may as easily become inordinate in its passion for order, as may the various
forces in the community in their passion for freedom, it is necessary to preserve a proper balance
between both principles, and to be as ready to
champion the individual against the community
as the community against the individual. Any definition of a proper balance between freedom and
order must always be at least slightly colored by
the exigencies of the moment which may make the
peril of the one seem greater and the security of
the other therefore preferable. Thus even the moral
and social principle which sets limits upon freedom
and order must, in a free society, be subject to
constant re-examination. In our own society this

---

and from the simple fact that man is man, nothing else being taken into account." One of the facts about man as
man is that his vitalities may be elaborated in indeterminate
variety. That is the fruit of his freedom. Not all of these
elaborations are equally wholesome and creative. But it is very
difficult to derive "in a necessary fashion" the final rules of
his individual and social existence. It is this indeterminateness
and variety which makes analogies between the "laws of nature" in the exact sense of the words and laws of human
nature, so great a source of confusion. It is man's nature to
transcend nature and to elaborate his own historical existence
in indeterminate degree.

re-examination has actually been too long delayed. That is why economic forces which come within an ace of dominating the community are able to prevent communal control of their power by appealing to traditional conceptions of liberty.

V

Though the individual is organically related to the community there is a point in human freedom where the individual transcends both his own community and the total historical process. Modern democratic theory has been too secular to understand or measure this full height of human self-transcendence. That is why it tends to oscillate between an individualism which makes the individual his own end, and a collectivism which regards the community as the end of the individual.

The ultimate transcendence of the individual over communal and social process can be understood and guarded only in a religious culture which knows of a universe of meaning in which this individual freedom has support and significance. When, in ancient empires, the religious interpretations of life became too purely political, as for instance in the Re worship of Egypt, new religions emerged, as the immortality cult of Horus and Osiris, in which individuals found some final meaning and fulfillment of life beyond the vicissitudes of the political situation.

In the Christian tradition of the West, Catholic Christianity has always insisted that man had a dimension which required freedom of conscience beyond all laws and requirements of the human community. In Catholicism this ultimate freedom was qualified by the fact that its conditions were defined and circumscribed by a religio-historical institution which was anchored in and partly dominated the very political community from which it required this freedom.

Thus an institutional restraint was placed upon the final freedom of the individual. Protestantism rebelled against these ultimate restraints and demanded a more complete individual freedom in the religious realm. This Protestant individualism is sometimes interpreted as no more than a religious rationalization of bourgeois individualism. It cannot be denied that the bourgeois desire for social freedom and the Protestant impulse to freedom against the inclusive and authoritative church contained points of relevance in thought and developed points of concurrence in history. But in one

respect they were very different. Protestant religious individualism was so transcendently conceived that Luther, at any rate, denied that it had
any relation to social freedom and he was inclined
to suggest that the possession of the one obviated
the necessity of the other. Calvinism and sectarian
Christianity on the other hand derived their demand for "civil liberty" from the assurance of
"evangelical liberty."

The real fact is that the final religious transcendence of the individual over the community is
both relevant and finally irrelevant to the social
process and to communal responsibilities.

Mystic forms of religion may seek to abstract
individual consciousness completely from the social
context in which it stands and to withdraw it from
the social responsibilities and distractions which
limit and discipline the individual. But in historical
faiths such as Christianity, the religious transcendence of the individual over the community is a final
resource for the highest forms of social realization.
The individual who declares with St. Paul, "to me
it is a small thing to be judged of men. . . . He
who judges me is the Lord," and who appeals to
a higher authority than the community's approval
or disapproval is not thereby emancipated from

communal responsibility. On the contrary the uneasy conscience which he experiences in commun-
ion with God reveals the social character of his
existence. He feels guilty because he has made his
life its own end and has not obeyed the command-
ment, "Thou shalt love the Lord thy God . . . and
thy neighbour as thyself." While modern secularism
speaks naïvely about the sociological source of conscience, the most effective opponents of tyrannical
government are today, as they have been in the
past, men who can say, "We must obey God rather
than man." Their resolution is possible because
they have a vantage point from which they can
discount the pretensions of demonic Cæsars and
from which they can defy malignant power as embodied in a given government.

Furthermore the final resource against idolatrous
national communities, who refuse to acknowledge
any law beyond their power, must be found in the
recognition of universal law by individuals, who
have a source of moral insight beyond the partial
and particular national communities, which are
always inclined to set a premature limit upon man's
sense of moral obligation. No world community can
ever be created if the full religious height of the

individual's freedom over the community is not explored and defended. An ultimate paradox of the moral life is that the same nation, which seems so universal, majestic and final from the perspective of the individual in the dimension of his social existence, is so limited and so bound to nature-necessity from the perspective of the individual's final freedom. From this height he surveys the ages, knows of ends and beginnings in history of which the nation knows nothing, and aspires to a purity of life which makes the actual community a constant source of frustration as well as fulfillment.

The sensitive individual has purer and broader ideals of brotherhood than any which are realized in any actual community. There is therefore a constant tension between individual conscience and the moral ambiguities of communities. In them social cohesion is always partly maintained by the denial of brotherhood. This tension persuades some mystics to flee to the quiet and purity of the inner world; and it prompts some utopians to seek the complete elimination of all moral ambiguities from historic existence. The one alternative is false and the other impossible. Rightly directed the tension between the individual conscience and the realities in actual communities can be a constant source of power for purifying and broadening the justice and brotherhood of the community.

Yet the individual whose freedom over natural process makes history possible, and whose freedom over history creates indeterminate new possibilities in it, has a final pinnacle of freedom where he is able to ask questions about the meaning of life which call the meaning of the historical process itself into question. The individual may ask with the Fourth Ezra: "How does it profit—that there is foretold an imperishable hope, whereas we are brought so miserably to futility?"[9] That is to say, he will recognize that his own life is not completely fulfilled by its organic relation to a social process pointing to some ultimate fulfillment beyond his life.

These profound questions about life from the perspective of the individual who is able to see the whole history of his nation (and of all nations for that matter) as a flux in time, imply eternity. Only a consciousness which transcends time can define and circumscribe the flux of time. The man who searches after both meaning and fulfillments beyond the ambiguous fulfillments and frustrations

[9]Fourth Ezra 7:120.

of history exists in a height of spirit which no historical process can completely contain. This height is not irrelevant to the life of the community, because new richness and a higher possibility of justice come to the community from this height of awareness. But the height is destroyed by any community which seeks prematurely to cut off this pinnacle of individuality in the interest of the community's peace and order. The problem of the individual and the community cannot be solved at all if the height is not achieved where the sovereign source and end of both individual and communal existence are discerned, and where the limits are set against the idolatrous self-worship of both individuals and communities.

CHAPTER THREE

THE COMMUNITY AND PROPERTY

I

E VERY RELATION between persons ultimately involves the questions of possessions. The "I"
is so intimately related to the "mine" and the
"thou" to the "thine" that relations of accord or
conflict between individuals usually imply questions of property. When life is very intimately related to life, as for instance in the family, questions
of mine and thine are resolved in a sense of common possessions. Tension between persons, on the
other hand, usually expresses itself in a sharpening
of the sense of unique and distinctive possessions,
which are carefully defined in order to discourage
the other from taking advantage of the self.

The collective tensions of society may be created
by ethnic rivalries and competing power impulses.

They are not as universally economic in origin as Marxism assumes. But questions of ownership and economic power are usually involved in them, even when they are not primary. The class conflicts of human history are, on the whole, contests between those who have, and those who lack, economic power, the latter of whom are driven by want, hunger and resentment to challenge the power of the economic overlords. These conflicts may not be overt; but they have not been absent in any society. They have become, however, increasingly overt and acrimonious in modern industrial society.

The agrarian societies of the past were not devoid of class conflict. There were slave revolts in Greece and Rome; and the friction between the patrician and plebeian classes of Rome was typical of the rivalries in many civilizations between classes which held various forms and degrees of economic power. But no traditional societies suffered from as acrimonious a debate on the property issue as has modern democratic society. This was partly due to the fact that the poor of ancient societies had no power with which to challenge their overlords, while the modern poor have at least the power inherent in their manipulation of the technical instruments of production. They can withhold their labor and, by this negative weapon of the strike, wrest some concessions from the economically powerful. Furthermore democracy has endowed them with the political power of suffrage, so that they can bring pressure to bear upon economic society through their power in political society.

But an added reason for the acrimony of the modern class conflict lies in the fact that the issue between the classes has become something more than the question of an equitable distribution of property. It is the issue about the very legitimacy of the right of property. On this issue there is little, or no, common ground between the middle classes, who regard property as the fruit of virtue and the guarantor of justice, and the industrial classes, who have come to think of the institution of property as the root of all evil in man and of all injustice in society.

Whenever a community faces an issue without any common ground between opposing forces, the resulting social friction may attain the proportions of a civil war. It is significant that modern democratic communities have been threatened by, or involved in, civil war, with the property issue as the crux of the conflict, despite the official democratic presupposition of a natural harmony be-

tween the various classes of society. This civil war
contributed to the disaster of Germany and France
and complicated the task of defending civilization
against Nazi tyranny; for the Nazi cynics were
successful in their initial political warfare against
civilization because they were able to beguile first
the propertied classes, and then the propertyless,
as their allies within the nations they intended to
destroy.

In Britain and the Scandinavian countries the
civil conflict on the property issue was mitigated
because older conceptions of property, derived from
an agrarian and feudal world, qualified both the
extravagant individualism of the bourgeois classes
and the doctrinaire collectivism of the industrial
workers. In America, and probably also in Holland, the tension between the classes never reached
the overt proportions which were manifested in
Germany and France, partly because the bourgeois
ethos was so powerful in these nations that the
labouring classes were unable to develop an effective challenge to its perspectives. Nevertheless the
whole of the western world has felt the effect of
this acrimonious debate. The world war has post-
poned, but not solved, the issues which underlie
it. These issues will harass each national commu-

nity as it seeks for social peace after the war, and they will also complicate the problems of the world community; for they are responsible for the religious hatred and affection which various groups have for Russia, the one nation in which the creed of proletarian rebels against private property has been actualized.

According to the creed of democratic liberalism the right of property is one of the "inalienable" rights, guaranteed by natural law. In Marxist thought the emergence of private property represents a kind of "Fall" in the history of mankind. All social evils are traced to this root source of evil. The present world crisis may well discredit the Marxist, as well as the liberal, credo, despite the rise of Russia as a world power. But our democratic world will not quickly resolve the conflict and social tension which have been created by these opposing views of property.

The conflict has been a long while in the making. Marxist and liberal property theories had their inception in the sixteenth century, when the Reformation generated two opposing views of property, which destroyed the circumspection of the classical Christian theory. According to the Christian theory (which was partly borrowed from Stoic thought, when it became necessary for the Christian movement to come to terms with the exigencies of politics and economics), property, as well as government, is a necessary evil, required by the Fall of man. The Christian, as the Stoic, theory presupposes an ideal possibility of a perfect accord between life and life which would make a sharp distinction between "mine" and "thine" unnecessary. The sinful selfishness of men, however, had destroyed this ideal possibility and made exclusive possession the only safeguard against the tendency of men to take advantage of one another. Such a theory has the advantage of viewing the "right" of property with circumspection and of justifying it only relatively and not absolutely. It was justified as an expedient tool of justice. The right of possession was not regarded in early Christian thought as a natural extension of the power of the person but rather as a right of defense against the inordinate claims of others.[1]

---

[1]Even this circumspect justification of property was too much for some of the early Fathers particularly in the East. Chrysostum declared: "The wealth is common to thee and to thy fellow servants, just as the sun is common, the earth, the air and all the rest. To grow rich without injustice is impossible." Proudhon's dictum "property is theft," had in other words an early Christian source.

St. Basil was equally emphatic: "Why are you rich and that man poor?" he asked. "You make your own things given you

Even before orthodox Protestantism accepted property distinctions uncritically, Catholic thought had gradually made less of the ideal possibility of common property (as symbolized in the perfection before the Fall) and accepted private property as either a requirement of the natural law or as an inevitable supplement of positive law.[2]

In Pope Leo XIII's encyclical *Rerum Novarum* property is defined as a necessity, in terms which can hardly be distinguished from those of eighteenth-century liberalism, though it must be observed that in Catholic thought economic power

---

to distribute. The coat which you preserve in your wardrobe belongs to the naked; the bread you keep belongs to the hungry. The gold you have hidden in the ground belongs to the needy."

The Eastern Church thus had a radical property ethic which was subordinated, however, to the theory that property is a necessary evil, until it emerged again in the sixteenth century as the sectarian property ethic.

[2]Thomas Aquinas justifies the right of property as follows: "[To possess property] is necessary for human life for three reasons: First, because man is more careful to procure what is for himself alone than that which is common to many or to all; . . . secondly, because human affairs are conducted in a more orderly fashion if each man is charged with taking care of some particular thing himself. . . . Thirdly, a more peaceful state is assured . . . if each man is content with his own." *Summa Theologica,* II. ii, q. 66. art. 2.

St. Thomas declares that "division of possession is not according to natural law but arose from human agreements which belong to positive law; . . . hence ownership of possessions is not contrary to natural law but an addition thereto." *Ibid.* The argument follows the thought of Aristotle.

always remains under political discipline and moral authority and is not granted the autonomy which eighteenth-century liberalism demanded. Pope Leo wrote: "The common opinion of mankind, little affected by a few dissident voices, has found in a careful study of nature and the laws of nature, the foundations of a division of property; and the practice of all the ages has consecrated the principle of private ownership as being pre-eminently in conformity with human nature and as conducing in an unmistakable manner to the peace and tranquility of human existence."

The difference in emphasis between this doctrine and the original doctrine of the Fathers is explained by a modern Catholic theologian as follows: "Great confusion has been caused by socialist writers who conclude, because they have read in some of the works of the Fathers that property did not exist by natural law, that it was therefore condemned as an illegitimate institution. Nothing could be more erroneous. The Fathers meant by these passages that in the state of nature, in the idealized Golden Age of the Pagans and the Garden of Eden of the Christians, there was no individual ownership of goods. The very moment however that men fell from this ideal state, communism became impossible. . . . To this extent it is right to say that the Fathers regarded property with disapproval. It was one of the institutions rendered necessary by the fall. . . . Property must be respected as one of the institutions which put a curb on his [man's] avarice."[3] This explanation is partly valid but fails to explain why Catholic thought, since the later Middle Ages, tends to omit mention of the ideal possibility of a propertyless state. By this omission Christian economic theory is subtly changed; for it gives property an absolute, rather than a relative, sanction.

It remained however for orthodox Protestant-ism, particularly Calvinism, to accept property distinctions without scruple or discrimination. In the case of Calvin this uncritical acceptance of property was due to his excessive determinism. Since property existed, he was certain that it must be by the will of God.[4] Calvinism did not, of course, emancipate the administration of property from all moral restraint, as was done in *laissez-faire* the-

---

[3]George Obrien, *An Essay on Medieval Economic Thought.*

[4]Calvin declared: "Though some seem to enrich themselves by vigilance it is nevertheless God who blesses and cares for them. Though others are rich before they are born and their fathers have acquired great possessions, this is nevertheless not by accident but the providence of God rules over it." "Sermon on Deut.." *Works,* XXVI. 627.

ory; the Christian idea that we are God's stewards of all we possess remained a force in Calvinistic as in Catholic thought. But the idea of stewardship easily degenerated into the idea of philanthropy as a justification for property distinctions. "Why then," said Calvin, "does God permit some to be rich and others poor on earth if not that he wants to give us an occasion to do good?"[5] Thus Calvinism laid the foundation for the hypocrisies of bourgeois and plutocratic idealism in which charity became a screen for injustice. These hypocrisies deserve all the strictures which have been levelled against them by sixteenth-century sectarianism and Marxism.

If both orthodox Catholicism and orthodox Protestantism tended to give a more and more uncritical justification of property, in which the early Christian scruples were forgotten, the sectarian Christianity of the sixteenth and seventeenth centuries, in which social revolt was combined with religious rebellion against feudalism, laid the foundation for the property ethic which finally culminated in the Marxist theory. The Anabaptists of the Continent and the Diggers of England were equalitarian and communist. They believed it pos-

---

[5] *Works*. XXVII. 337.

sible to restore the original state of man's innocency and they thought that the primary method of this restoration was the return to primitive communism. The Anabaptists taught "that a Christian must not possess anything proper to himself but that whatever he has he must make common." Gerard Winstanley, leader of the Diggers of the Cromwellian period in England, anticipated practically every facet of the Marxist creed. "The earth," he declared, "was made by Almighty God to be a common treasury of livelihood for the whole of mankind." This state of common ownership was destroyed when "our ancestors by the sword first did murder their fellow creatures and then after plunder and steal their land."[6]

Winstanley was half Christian and half Marxist in his interpretation of the rise of evil. Sometimes he declared that sin arose through the development of "particular love" which destroyed the perfection of "universal love" and brought private possession in its train as the first fruit of evil. Sometimes he reversed the process and, as in Marxism, made the inception of private property the root, rather than the fruit, of evil: "This particular propriety of mine

---

[6]From Winstanley's "Declaration of the Poor Oppressed People."

and thine," he declared, "has brought all the misery upon the people."

Against the conservative idea that property may be the fruit of diligence Winstanley presents a telling argument: "No man can be rich, but he must be rich by his own labours or by the labours of other men helping him. If a man has no help from his neighbours he shall never gather an estate of hundreds and thousands a year. If other men help him then are those riches his neighbours' as well as his own."

The economic viewpoints of Calvinism on the one hand and of the sectarian Christians, as typified by Winstanley on the other, thus contain the seeds of the contradictory opinions on property which have divided the democratic world from the sixteenth to the present centuries. Even the modern class conflict, in which these ideas are the weapons of opposing classes, was anticipated in the sixteenth and seventeenth centuries; for Calvinism was on the whole the religion of the middle classes and sectarianism was the religion of the disinherited.

But modern secularism, both liberal and Marxist, has set property theories in even more complete contradiction to each other. Liberal thought tended

to emancipate property relations from all political
control or moral restraint which Christian thought
always maintained. Marxist philosophy on the
other hand derived all historic evil from the rise
of private property more completely than sectarian
Christianity. Thus secularism removed the last common denominator between opposing convictions on
the question of property.

Ideas, as weapons of social conflict, have no in-
dependent potency. We must therefore not assume
that a reconsideration of the ideas would eliminate
the conflict. But democratic society must find some
common denominator in this debate. If history has
actually refuted some of the illusions in both the
liberal and the Marxist theories of property, it is
important to record these lessons of history. This
would serve to mitigate the class struggle and reduce it to proportions which would not threaten
the whole democratic process.

II

The bourgeois notions about property contain
two errors, closely related to each other. The one
error is the excessive individualism of the bourgeois property concept, which is part and parcel

of a general exaggeration of individual freedom in middle-class existence. The other error is contained in the prevailing presupposition of liberal thought that property represents primarily an ordinate and defensive power to be used against the inclination of others to take advantage of the self. The fact is that property, as every other form of power, cannot be limited to the defensive purpose. If it grows strong enough it becomes an instrument of aggression and usurpation. These two errors must be considered more fully.

Bourgeois ideas of property participated in the generally excessive individualism of middle-class life. Just as the individual does not have as discrete an existence as is assumed in liberal thought, so also is it impossible to draw as sharp distinctions between "mine" and "thine" as liberal property ideas imply. One reason for the acrimony of the conflict on property in the modern world is that this individualism was introduced into history at the beginning of the very epoch which would develop highly collective forms of commercial and industrial wealth. There is thus a serious gulf between social function of modern property and the emphasis upon its "private" character in legal tradition and social thought.

Sometimes the individualism of liberal property theories is derived from the fact that the intricacies and complexities of a commercial and industrial civilization were simply not anticipated in the early period of our epoch. John Locke significantly draws his justification of property from a consideration of the simplest agricultural economy.

For Locke property is primarily an extension of the power of the person. "Every man," he declares, "has a 'property' in his own 'person.' . . . The 'labour' of his body, and the 'work' of his hands, we may say, are properly his. Whosoever, then, he removes out of the state that nature hath provided, and left it in, he hath mixed his labour with, and joined to it something that is his own, and thereby makes it his property."[7]

This theory has the merit of being historically correct in tracing the rise of property in primitive society. When Locke declares, "The law of reason makes the deer that Indian's who hath killed it," he is describing a historic development which anthropological research has since validated, though Locke's theory does not do justice to the communistic elements in the hunting period of society and

[7]John Locke, *Two Treatises of Government,* Book II, ch. v, par. 27.

to the vestigial communism in the pastoral period. The deer did not always belong to the Indian who killed it, or the whale to the person who dragged it to the shore. It was frequently made available to the whole tribe. But it is true that the individual usually did establish some special and exclusive claim by the right of his labour, however minimal.

But a description of the genesis of an institution is no adequate definition of its true character. In Locke's own day economic life was already too complex and many economic activities were already too mutual to permit as exact an isolation of the labour of each person as his theory implied.

Sometimes the individualism of bourgeois property concepts is consciously related to the experience of a commercial civilization. This experience was particularly fertile in hiding the social function of property behind its individualistic tokens.

In terms of its individual accessibility and manageability, commercial property is more liquid and mobile than property in land. Stocks and bonds and certificates of indebtedness can be stuffed into a drawer and can be transferred without the difficulties which attend the transfer of property in land. Yet these papers are tokens of something more substantial, of banks and commercial establishments, of insurance companies and all kinds of properties which represent intricate and complex mutual functions in society. The bourgeois mind, from the earliest to the present day, has been the victim of illusions caused by the contrast between the private character of its "tokens" of property and the social character of the real wealth which these tokens and counters signify.

Sometimes the individualism of liberal theory is derived from the earliest experiences of capitalistic development, which has been refuted by later experience. The moral justification of dividends in classical economics, for instance, is based upon the experience of budding capitalism. Dividends are regarded as the reward for abstention from immediate satisfactions and as a necessary incentive for building up working capital by prompting individuals to abstemiousness in refraining from the consumption of the rewards of their toil. Actually many a commercial and industrial enterprise was thus initiated by the savings of diligent and thrifty individuals. But a profitable enterprise may soon bring in such large returns that it makes both saving and extravagant consumption possible. The fact that the labour of many, besides the original owners, contributes to the returns is obscured in the individualistic conception of savings and investment.

The most glaring contradiction between bourgeois individualism and the social function of property became apparent as commercial civilization was gradually transmuted into an industrial society in which collective production became the primary source of wealth. The modern factory is a great collective process. Technical advance has made it impossible for the worker to own either his own tools or the place of his work. Both the wealth represented by the machine and the wealth which the machine produces are generated by complex mutual services. The "private" ownership of such a process is anachronistic and incongruous; and the individual control of such centralized power is an invitation to injustice.

It is this incongruity between the social tradition and the actual function of industrialized property in modern life which has accentuated social tensions in our society. The Marxist creed has merely been the instrument of this tension and not its creator. The Marxist program for the socialization of productive property involves some difficulties which were not anticipated in Marxist thought for reasons which we must discuss presently. It must be apparent, however, that a theory emphasizing the social character of industrial property is closer to the truth than the bourgeois creed which insists on its individual character. Modern industrial communities have in fact been forced to subject economic process to more and more political control. The stakes of the entire community in the process were so obvious that the logic of the situation overcame the dogmas upon which modern capitalism was founded. Every modern democratic society has been prompted, both by its natural necessities and by the prompting of the voting power of the workers, to redress economic inequalities through the use of political power. This process has invalidated the Marxist thesis that the state is merely the executive committee of the possessing classes. On the other hand this use of political power has not been sufficient to save modern industrial communities from industrial crises, occasioned by the great disproportion of economic power in the community. This disproportion results in a dynamic form of injustice which not only affronts the conscience of the community but also interferes with the industrial process; for too much wealth is heaped up for capital investments and too little is distributed for consumption. A part of the Marxist interpretation of the situation therefore has been validated by history.

The fact that the Marxist conception of the social character of productive property is clearly nearer to the truth than the bourgeois notions will unfortunately not prevent the privileged classes, particularly in America, from seeking to defy the lessons of history. America is probably the only nation in which a serious effort will be made to restore the purer individualism of the past. In Britain, the birthplace of classical liberalism, the chasm between the Conservative Party, in which older, feudal conceptions of property prevail, and the Labour Party, which is informed by a qualified Marxism, is not as deep as between the opposing forces in America. This is true despite the fact that there is no religious devotion to Marxist creeds in America. What America gains by the lack of a too dogmatic Marxism, it loses by the anachronism of a too dogmatic and consistent liberalism and individualism. This is a consequence of the fact that the wealth, security and vast expanse of America gave bourgeois illusions a greater force in the United States than in any other nation. We must therefore expect more social friction and convulsion in the settlement of this issue than in Britain. The international position of Britain may be more precarious than our own; but her domestic peace and order are more secure.

III

Though Marxism is nearer to the truth than liberalism on the property issue, the socialization of property as proposed in Marxism is too simple a solution of the problem. An analysis of the Marxist error reveals a curious affinity between Marxism and liberalism, despite their contradictory conceptions of property. Liberalism and Marxism share a common illusion of the "children of light." Neither understands property as a form of power which can be used in either its individual or its social form as an instrument of particular interest against the general interest. Liberalism makes this mistake in regard to private property and Marxism makes it in regard to socialized property.

The bourgeois idea of property participates in the general error of liberalism: its belief that all individual power, whether in the political or the economic sphere, is ordinate, limited and primarily defensive. John Locke limited the power of property by definition. A man's property was the part of nature with which he had "mixed his labour." The limit of his labour was therefore the limit of his property. "The measure of property nature has well set," he declares, "by the extent of men's labour and the conveniency of life. No man's labour could subdue or appropriate all, nor could his enjoyment consume more than a small part; so that it was impossible for any man this way to entrench upon the right of another or acquire to himself a property, to the prejudice of his neighbour."[8]

Locke was quite conscious of the fact that history had elaborated the early property relations; that by "the appropriation of land" and the extension of trade through the invention of money, property had ceased to be limited and fairly equal in distribution. Locke had, in fact, his own conception of a state of innocency, a period "before the desire of having more than men needed had altered the intrinsic value of things."[9] It was in the "state of nature," which in Marxism is described as a state of communism, that, according to Locke, all men had strictly limited property rights, which

---

[8]*Ibid.,* Book II, ch. v, par. 36.
[9]*Ibid.,* 37.

did not infringe upon the rights of the neighbour. Locke realized that in "civil society" the natural balance of the state of nature is destroyed. That is why civil government becomes necessary, the primary function of which is to "preserve the property" of each member because he can no longer preserve it by his own right, having "quitted his power to punish offenses against the law of nature in prosecution of his own private judgment."[10]

This is no *laissez-faire* theory. Locke does not believe in an automatic balance in economic relations as the physiocrats did a century later. At the same time he does not fully understand how inordinate and disproportionate economic power may become. He thinks of the political state, functioning as an umpire and preserving each man's power of property against the undue power of others. He does not anticipate a situation in which property may become so social and its power so centralized and inordinate that the very institution of property may require reconstruction.

In later physiocratic and *laissez-faire* theory it is assumed that property, interest on wealth, wages and every other element in the economic process are held in automatic balance by the free market

------

[10]*Ibid.*, ch. vii, par. 88.

and competition. This theory left the important
fact out of account, that every economic process
begins with a disproportion of economic power.
Some men have land and some have not. Some
gain a foothold in the commercial and industrial
process and others do not. Modern technical civilization accentuates, rather than diminishes, these
disproportions of economic power. This fact, which
Ricardo first saw and which Marx explored more
fully, invalidates the basic presuppositions of liberal ideas of property. The development from competitive to monopoly capitalism is the historic refutation of the idea that property is primarily an
ordinate and defensive power to be used against
the inclinations of others to take advantage of the
self. Property, like every other form of power, is
both defensive and offensive; and no sharp line can
be drawn between its two functions. It is defensive
only so long as the individual possesses so little of
it, that he will not be tempted to use it for domination over others.

In a sense the disproportions of economic power,
accentuated rather than mitigated in modern technical society, refute the early Christian, as well as
the bourgeois, property ethic. For the early Christian theory assumed that property was a necessity

of defense against the sins of others and failed to appreciate to what degree it was an instrument of the sin of the self against others less favoured with economic power.

Once it is fully understood that there are no natural harmonies and equilibria of power in history, as there are in nature, and that advancing civilization tends to accentuate, rather than diminish, such disproportions of power as exist in even primitive communities, it must become apparent that property rights become instruments of injustice. In that sense the Marxist interpretation of the effect of property in history is correct. Yet the Marxist solution for the problem of property is involved in merely another version of the older liberal illusion. Marxism assumes that the socialization of property will destroy all disproportions of economic power in the community. It looks for that perfect equilibrium of power on the other side of the revolution, which liberal theory imagines as a characteristic of the economic process in present society. Marxism does not understand that even universalized property may become the instrument of particular interest.

The Marxist illusion is partly derived from a romantic conception of human nature. It thinks that the inclination of men to take advantage of each other is a corruption which was introduced into history by the institution of property. It therefore assumes that the socialization of property will eliminate human egotism. Its failure to understand the perennial and persistent character of human egotism in any possible society, prompts it to make completely erroneous estimates of human behaviour on the other side of a revolution.

A second source of Marxist illusions is its belief that the ownership of property is the sole and only source of economic power. The management and manipulation of industrial process represents social power. Such power remains subordinate to the power of ownership in a capitalistic society,[11] but it naturally grows in any society in which the rights of private ownership have been destroyed. The development of a managerial class in Russia, combining economic with political power, is an historic refutation of the Marxist theory. In recent years there has been a tendency of industrial technicians, who derived political prestige from technical competence, to supplant managers who achieved

[11]The power of the manager is not as great as James Burnham pretends in his *The Managerial Revolution*. He has nevertheless rendered a service in analyzing the increasing power of the manager in a technical society.

industrial positions through political prestige.[12]

The Marxist theory fails to anticipate the inevitable rise of an oligarchy in a new society, partly because it has utopian ideas of idyllic relations in such a society, which obviate the necessity of the use of any form of coercive power; and partly because it identifies economic power too absolutely with the power of private ownership.

The theory does of course provide for a provisional political oligarchy, "the dictatorship of the proletariat." But nowhere in Marxist thought is the combination of political and economic power in the hands of this oligarchy understood. Nor are any provisions made to place restraints upon its political power; for the utopianism of Marxism generates the illusion that the ultimate universal victory of communism will gradually obviate the necessity of every form of political coercion, including of course the coercion of the provisional dictatorship.

These illusions are the perfect fruits of the stupidity of the children of light and reveal the affinities, under the differences, between Marxist and bourgeois universalism. Bourgeois property theory

---

[12]For a careful analysis of this development see *Management in Russian Industry and Agriculture* by Gregory Bienstock, Solomon Schwartz and Aaron Yugow. (Oxford Press.)

has no safeguard against the power of individual
property; and Marxist theory has no protection
against the excessive power of those who manipu-
late a socialized economic process or who combine
the control of both the economic and the political
process.

Even if a community approached the socialization of property by gradual stages and circum-
vented the period of revolution and dictatorship,
it would still face the question of how to socialize
property without creating pools of excessive social
power in the hands of those who manage both
its economic and political processes. A community
which preserved its democratic institutions in the
area of politics, while it socialized its large-scale
industrial property, would have the advantage of
preserving a democratic check upon the power of
economic managers. Yet their power might be so
great that they could use it to establish control
over the political institutions.

A full analysis of these complexities must invali-
date any simple solution of the problem of property. Since economic power, as every other form
of social power, is a defensive force when possessed
in moderation and a temptation to injustice when
it is great enough to give the agent power over

others, it would seem that its widest and most equitable distribution would make for the highest degree of justice. This gives a provisional justification
to the liberal theory. But bourgeois liberalism assumes a natural equilibrium of economic power in
the community which historic facts refute. If the
economic process is left severely alone either the
strong devour the weak, in which case monopoly
displaces competition, or competition breeds chaos
in the community. The anarchy of competition in
a modern situation of technical interdependence
sometimes forces the community to encourage
rather than destroy the unification of economic
process (in public utilities for instance) in order
to avoid the competitive waste. The tendency toward monopoly is obviously a concomitant of the
general increase of interdependence in communal
relations in a technical society. In so far as the
unification of technical process is a service to the
community (despite the perils of centralization of
power which inhere in it), the effort to destroy
the unification in order to avoid its concomitant
perils,[13] would seem as unwise and futile as the
analogous effort of peasants of a previous age to

---

[13]As in the Sherman anti-trust laws and in anti-chain store
legislation.

prevent the use of machinery upon the land. The community must find a way of dealing with the problem of centralized power without destroying the unity and efficiency of the process. The social ownership of the power and wealth, derived from unified process, is certainly more plausible than the effort to maintain its individual character in defiance of inexorable historical developments. Yet it may be wise for the community to sacrifice something to efficiency for the sake of preserving a greater balance of forces and avoiding undue centralization of power.

This is the kind of question which cannot be solved once for all. The contrasting perils of anarchy and injustice, arising from too little and too much equilibrium of economic power, or from too much or too little social control of it, must be considered in the light of each new situation and technical development. The property issue must, in other words, be continually solved within the framework of the democratic process. In attempting proximate solutions certain distinctions in types of property are valuable without being final. It is valuable to remember that some forms of property are by their very nature power over others, while other types are primarily the power to secure the person against the aggrandizement of others or against the caprice of life and nature; and again others represent primarily the power to perform one's social function. Yet modern civilization has developed socialized processes in defiance of these distinctions. A workman's tool is the most obvious form of the extension of personal power. It is an aid for the performance of his function. But the tool has become too big for the worker to own. The home is the most obvious form of property as individual security; and yet the multiple dwellings of urban communities have placed the home beyond the reach of individual ownership.

Property in land is both individual security and an instrument for the performance of function. Individual ownership in land, therefore, has a moral justification which dogmatic collectivists have never understood. Yet landlordism is the most ancient form of oppression and the effects of a technical civilization have not left agriculture unaffected. Mechanization tends toward large-scale agricultural production; and large-scale production tends to destroy the small owner unless he learns to develop voluntary cooperation in the use of large-scale machinery. Many solutions depend upon the degree of resourcefulness with which new situations are met and cannot be determined abstractly.

While the intensity and extent of technical interdependence have invalidated bourgeois conceptions of property and have placed the logic of history behind proposals for socialization, the logic is not unambiguous. Since there are no forms of the socialization of property which do not contain some peril of compounding economic and political power, a wise community will walk warily and test the effect of each new adventure before further adventures.

There must, in other words, be a continuous debate on the property question in democratic society and a continuous adjustment to new developments. Such a debate is possible, however, only if there is some common denominator between opposing factions.

The contradictory dogmas about property can be most easily dissolved if the utopianism which underlies both of them, is dispelled. In communities, such as America, where the Marxist dogma has never developed the power to challenge the bourgeois one, the primary requirement of justice is that the dominant dogma be discredited. The

obvious facts about property which both liberal and
Marxist theories have obscured are: that all property is power; that some forms of economic power
are intrinsically more ordinate than others and
therefore more defensive, but that no sharp line
can be drawn between what is ordinate and what
is inordinate; that property is not the only form of
economic power and that the destruction of private property does not therefore guarantee the
equalization of economic power in a community;
that inordinate power tempts its holders to abuse
it, which means to use it for their own ends; that
the economic, as well as the political, process requires the best possible distribution of power for
the sake of justice and the best possible management of this equilibrium for the sake of order.

None of these propositions solves any specific
issue of property in a given instance. But together
they set the property issue within the framework
of democratic procedure. For democracy is a
method of finding proximate solutions for insolu-
ble problems.

CHAPTER FOUR

DEMOCRATIC TOLERATION AND THE GROUPS OF THE COMMUNITY

I

CONTRARY TO THE BELIEF and expectations of eighteenth-century democrats, a national community is both integrated and divided by many ethnic, cultural, religious and economic groups. Early democratic idealists were too individualistic to appreciate the creative character of these groups or to anticipate the perennial peril of disunity which might arise from them. The founding fathers of America regarded "faction" as an unmitigated evil. The American Constitution was designed to prevent the emergence of the very political parties without which it has become impossible to maintain our democratic processes. Of our early constitutionalists, Madison was realistic enough to recognize the inevitability of factions. But even he tried in every way to circumscribe their development.

The individualism of the eighteenth century is rather curious in the light of the experience of the seventeenth century. The democracy of England was essentially the achievement of that century. The cause of its emergence was the inability of the nation to solve the problem of cultural diversity on other than democratic terms. With the disintegration of the religious and social unity of the medieval period, the various economic and religious groups expressed each its own characteristic religious and economic convictions with great freedom. Most of them hoped to have their own position prevail within the entire nation; but none were strong enough to achieve this end. Of the religious groups only the Independents and Levellers genuinely believed in religious toleration. The others finally accepted it as the only solution for the variety of religious and cultural movements which had developed and which could not be brought back into the pattern of cultural uniformity.

Democracy is thus, in one sense, the fruit of a cultural and religious pluralism created by inexorable forces of history. The seventeenth century was in some respects the culmination of a long historical process which began with the first disintegration of the uniformity of the primitive tribe. In primitive life complete uniformity is a necessary prerequisite of communal unity. The more the imagination develops, the more it becomes possible and necessary to allow life to express itself variously within one community. However, the peril of disharmony from such variety is always so great and the pride of a dominant group within any community is so imperious, that some effort is always made to preserve a coerced unity, even after the forces of history have elaborated multifarious forms of culture. The Renaissance and Reformation represent the final emergence of this variety in our western world after centuries of medieval uniformity. The new wine of a humanistic science, of autonomous national cultures and of religious sectarianism could no longer be contained in the old bottles.

Catholics are fond of defining the Renaissance and Reformation as forces of decadence because they initiated the destruction of the unity of Christendom. The new freedom and variety which they established did indeed threaten the community with, and sometimes actually resulted in, chaos;

for chaos is a perennial peril of freedom; but, given a certain level of spiritual maturity, coerced uniformity is more decadent than freedom. Mature cultures must finally face the necessity of achieving communal harmony within the conditions of freedom. The Renaissance and Reformation ushered in a period of creativity rather than decadence; but it must be admitted that western history has been unable to avoid some forms of decadence arising from the new freedom, just as adolescents are not always able to cope with life after emancipation from the restraints of childhood.

Democratic institutions are the cause, as well as the consequence, of cultural variety and social pluralism. Once freedom is established, economic interests, cultural convictions and ethnic amalgams proliferate in ever greater degree of variety. Traditional communities were ethnically as well as religiously homogeneous. The stability of an agrarian economy held even class forces in a static equilibrium or disbalance. But when the religio-cultural unity was broken all other forces of variety were set in motion and became dynamic. Modern nations are no longer ethnically homogeneous though most of them do have a core of ethnic unity. Furthermore they all must contend with dynamic class forces. Class tensions may, and have, destroyed the very foundations of unity in some modern national communities. Yet the complexities of a technical civilization make it impossible to bring them back into the narrow confines of coerced unity. Democracy must find a way of allowing them to express themselves without destroying the unity and life of the community.

The profounder significance of Nazism lies in the fact that it sought to re-establish a primitive unity in the community. It did this with a remarkable degree of consistency; for it sought after a tribal homogeneity of race, a cultural unity upon the basis of a tribal religion and an economic unity through the creation of an omnipotent state, powerful enough to suppress all economic freedom. This Nazi effort was profound in the sense that the perils of liberty are sufficient to have made it practically inevitable that some community would try to avoid them in the manner of Nazism. But the effort was also significantly perverse. It is no more possible for a mature and highly elaborated community to return to the unity of its tribal simplicity than for a mature man to escape the perils of maturity by a return to childhood. The fact that primitivism results in perversity and that coerced unity produces sadistic cruelties (in place of the uncoerced unities of genuinely primitive life) is a tremendously valuable lesson for our civilization. It ought to teach us that we must go forward, and cannot go backward, in solving the problems with which higher forms of communal maturity present us.

The children of darkness in this case set the false universal of the national community against all other particular expressions of vitality; but a genuine universalism must seek to establish harmony without destroying the richness and variety of life. One of the greatest problems of democratic civilization is how to integrate the life of its various subordinate, ethnic, religious and economic groups in the community in such a way that the richness and harmony of the whole community will be enhanced and not destroyed by them.

II

It will be well to consider this task of democratic civilization in terms of the three primary types of groups: religious, ethnic and economic, by which the life of the community is both enriched and imperiled. Though religious controversies are not the most fertile sources of conflict in the community today it is well to consider the issue of cultural and religious pluralism first because religious diversity remains potentially the most basic source of conflict. Religious ideas and traditions may not be directly involved in the organization of a community. But they are the ultimate sources of the moral standards from which political principles are derived. In any case both the foundation and the pinnacle of any cultural structure are religious; for any scheme of values is finally determined by the ultimate answer which is given to the ultimate question about the meaning of life. This is true even of ostensibly secular cultures which covertly raise some contingent value of life into the position of the ultimate, and worship it as god. Religio-cultural diversity may prove the most potent source of communal discord because varying answers to the final question about the meaning of life produce conflicting answers on all proximate issues of moral order and political organization. The chasm between Mohammedanism and Hinduism is, for instance, the most serious hazard to the unity and freedom of India. Whenever religious and cultural diversity becomes geographically localized and so marked that interpenetration and mutual contact cease, the peril to the harmony of the community increases.

There are three primary approaches to the problem of religious and cultural diversity in the western world, the merits of which we ought to weigh in turn. The first is a religious approach (typified particularly by Catholicism) in which an effort is made to overcome religious diversity and restore the original unity of culture. The second is the approach of secularism which attempts to achieve cultural unity through the disavowal of traditional historical religions. The third is again a religious approach, which seeks to maintain religious vitality within the conditions of religious diversity.

Catholicism frankly accepts religious diversity in a national community only under the compulsion of history. In predominantly Catholic nations it insists on official status. In predominantly secular or Protestant nations it submits to the policy of a free church in a free state but regards this situation as provisional. Its doctrinal position is that the true religion is known and validated, and that it is the business of the state to support the true religion. In the words of Pope Leo XIII: "It is a sin in the state not to have care of religion . . . or out of the many forms of religion to adopt that one which chimes in with the fancy, for we are bound absolutely to worship God in that way which He hath shown to be His will."[1] According to the Catholic doctrine, "no state is justified in supporting error or in according error the same recognition as truth,"[2] the truth of course being embodied in the Catholic faith.

Obviously this position is in conflict with the presuppositions of a free society. Fathers John A. Ryan and Francis J. Boland warn Catholics against the error of denying or obscuring the force of this doctrine in the interest of assuaging the fears of non-Catholic democrats. They think it would be better policy to call attention to the fact that Catholicism does not claim the right to suppress dissident faiths if it happens to have merely a majority in a nation. It must have an overwhelming majority so that the suppression of dissidence will not imperil the public peace. This condition, Ryan and Boland argue, makes the possible application of Catholic policy so remote in a nation in which religious culture has become diversified "that no practical man will let it disturb his equanimity."[3]

---

[1] In the encyclical *Immortale Dei*.

[2] J. A. Ryan and F. J. Boland, *Catholic Principles of Politics*, p. 314.

[3] *Ibid.*, p. 321.

These Catholic teachers admit, in other words, that the official Catholic policy has become irrelevant to the situation of any modern nation in which religious diversity has become so fully developed that no religious uniformity could be achieved in any predictable future. It is significant, however, that the policy must be maintained despite its irrelevance. This reveals the chasm between the presuppositions of a free society and the inflexible authoritarianism of the Catholic religion.

Modern secularists, and some Protestants, regard the Catholic position as completely absurd. While it is in basic conflict with a democratic society, the weaknesses of the secular approach to the problem of religious diversity will always give the Catholic answer to the problem some degree of plausibility.

It is necessary, however, to consider the merits of the secular approach before considering its weaknesses. Modern national communities sometimes favour a secular state, without desiring a secularized community, because they believe that only such a state can prevent one religion from gaining official status. This was the position of Roger Williams, for instance, who was himself a pious sectarian Christian and whose theories of tolerance were, together with those of Thomas Jefferson, most influential in determining American doctrines of religious freedom. Sometimes, as was the case in eighteenth-century France, the secular state was the expression of a secular culture. American theories of religious tolerance stand somewhere between the French theories, which embody the convictions of a secularized culture, and English theories, in which religious freedom is achieved within the presuppositions of a Christian culture. All modern nations have, of course, become increasingly secularized. In America the original pattern was a secular state, favored by a sectarian (highly diversified) Christianity. The present pattern is that of a partially secularized community, favoring religious toleration, partly because it does not regard the religious convictions which create religious differences in the community as significant.

Pure secularism regards religious loyalties as outmoded forms of culture which will gradually disappear with the general extension of enlightened good-will. It looks forward to the cultural unification of the community upon the basis of a "common faith" embodied in the characteristic credos of bourgeois liberalism.[4]

---

[4]This is the position of the most typical and greatest philosopher of American secularism, John Dewey, as expressed in *A Common Faith*.

It must be admitted that toleration in religion could probably not have been achieved in any modern democratic society had there not been a considerable decay of traditional religious loyalties. Tolerance is the virtue of people who do not believe anything, said Gilbert Chesterton quite truly. There is an ideal possibility that people may hold ultimate religious convictions with a sufficient degree of humility to live amicably with those who have contradictory convictions. But religious humility is a rarer achievement than religious indifference. For this reason modern democratic toleration was made possible partly because a bourgeois culture had created a spirit of indifference toward the most characteristic affirmations of historic forms of religious faith. It is a question, however, whether the health of a culture can be maintained upon the basis of such a shallow unity.

The fact is that a theory of democratic toleration which enjoins provisional freedom for all religions in the hope that the bourgeois climate of opinion will gradually dissipate all religious convictions except the secularized bourgeois versions of them, is a typical fruit of the illusions of modern "children of light." They expect modern society to achieve an essential uniformity through the common con-

victions of "men of good-will" who have been enlightened by modern liberal education. This belief
fails to appreciate the endless variety of cultural
and religious convictions, growing out of varying
historical situations. It does not understand the
perennial power of particularity in human culture.
The most pathetic aspect of the bourgeois faith
is that it regards its characteristic perspectives and
convictions as universally valid and applicable, at
the precise moment in history when they are being
unmasked as the peculiar convictions of a special
class which flourished in a special situation in
western society.

The bourgeois culture which hoped to unify not
only western society but ultimately the whole of
human culture, expresses itself in two varieties,
each of which has its own difficulties in solving the
problem of diversity in ultimate religious convictions. In one of its forms bourgeois secularism is
itself a covert religion. In the other (and more sophisticated) form it represents a sceptical awareness of the relativity of all perspectives and the
finiteness of all human knowledge. In the more
naïve form, secularism is a covert religion which
believes that it has ultimate answers to life's ultimate problems. Its profoundest belief is that the

historical process is itself redemptive and guaran-
tees both the meaning of life and its fulfillment.
It believes, in short, in progress. There is indeed
progress in history in the sense that it presents us
with continually larger responsibilities and tasks.
But modern history is an almost perfect refutation
of modern faith in a redemptive history. History
is creative but not redemptive. The conquest of
nature, in which the bourgeois mind trusted so
much, enriches life but also imperils it. The increase
in the intensity and extent of social cohesion extends community, but also aggravates social conflict. The bourgeois surrogate for religion is, in
other words, a sorry affair.

Sometimes modern secularism expresses itself in
more modest religious terms. It holds that the end
of life is the creation of a democratic society. In
so far as a part of the meaning of life is created
and fulfilled in man's social relations, this form of
the secular faith is at least half true. But it is also
half false; because it fails to recognize that man
has the capacity and the necessity to transcend
every social and political process in which he is
involved and to ask ultimate questions about the
meaning of life for which there is no answer in the

partial fulfillments and frustrations of the historical process. To make a democratic society the end of human existence is a less vicious version of the Nazi creed. It is less vicious because democratic society allows criticism of its life and pretensions. It is thereby prevented from becoming completely idolatrous. The creed is nevertheless dangerous because no society, not even a democratic one, is great enough or good enough to make itself the final end of human existence.

In its more sophisticated form secularism represents a form of scepticism which is conscious of the relativity of all human perspectives. In this form it stands on the abyss of moral nihilism and threatens the whole of life with a sense of meaninglessness. Thus it creates a spiritual vacuum into which demonic religions easily rush. Continental varieties of secularism have on the whole taken this more sophisticated form; while American secularism has been more naïve and therefore, on the whole, less dangerous. The social and political problems of life have seemed so much more soluble in America that this nation was particularly prone to the illusion of a redemptive history. On the continent of Europe, on the other hand, life was too tragic to allow these sentimentalities to flourish. When therefore the sense of a tragic meaning of life, as expounded in the Christian faith, was dissipated, it gave way to a pure despair. Since no one can live in despair, the primitive and demonic religion of Nazism and extravagant nationalism filled the vacuum. In America the bourgeois mind has not yet faced the ultimate issues, nor been confronted with the inadequacy of its own credos. This is why the secularization of culture still seems an adequate answer in America for both the ultimate questions about the meaning of life and the immediate problem of the unity and harmony of our society.

There is a religious solution of the problem of religious diversity. This solution makes religious and cultural diversity possible within the presuppositions of a free society, without destroying the religious depth of culture. The solution requires a very high form of religious commitment. It demands that each religion, or each version of a single faith, seek to proclaim its highest insights while yet preserving an humble and contrite recognition of the fact that all actual expressions of religious faith are subject to historical contingency and relativity. Such a recognition creates a spirit of tolerance and makes any religious or cultural movement hesitant to claim official validity for its form of religion or to demand an official monopoly for its cult.

Religious humility is in perfect accord with the presuppositions of a democratic society. Profound religion must recognize the difference between divine majesty and human creatureliness; between the unconditioned character of the divine and the conditioned character of all human enterprise. According to the Christian faith the pride, which seeks to hide the conditioned and finite character of all human endeavour, is the very quintessence of sin. Religious faith ought therefore to be a constant fount of humility; for it ought to encourage men to moderate their natural pride and to achieve some decent consciousness of the relativity of their own statement of even the most ultimate truth. It ought to teach them that their religion is most certainly true if it recognizes the element of error and sin, of finiteness and contingency which creeps into the statement of even the sublimest truth.

Historically the highest form of democratic toleration is based upon these very religious insights. The real foundation of Anglo-Saxon toleration lies in the religious experience of seventeenth-century

England. In the religious conflicts of the Cromwellian period there were religious fanatics who were anxious to secure religious monopoly for their particular version of the Christian faith. There were also some secularists who hoped for toleration through the decay of religion. But the victory for toleration was really won by various groups of Christians, among which were the Independents and the Levellers, certain types of moderate Anglicans touched with Renaissance-humanistic perspectives, and some individuals in other sectarian groups. Their viewpoint was expressed in John Milton's *Areopagitica* and in John Saltmarsh's *Smoke in the Temple*. The latter perfectly expresses the religious humility which must form the basis of religious democracy: "Let us," he declares, "not assume any power of infallibility toward each other . . . for another's evidence is as dark to me as mine to him . . . till the Lord enlighten us both for discerning alike."

The achievement of communal harmony on the basis of secularism means the sacrifice of religious profundity as the price of a tolerable communal accord. It is a dangerous sacrifice; but it would be well for religious devotees who criticize secularism to recognize that it has sometimes been a necessary one. The fanaticism of the various religions and various versions of the same religion frequently made no other solution in the modern democratic state possible.

In Britain the heritage of the seventeenth century has been sufficiently vital to make it possible for that nation to attain religious liberty without secularizing its culture in the same degree as has been the case in France and America. In this achievement Britain also was favoured by the fact that religious diversity was not quite as marked as in the other nations. But the basic religious homogeneity of Britain, expressed in the dominant Presbyterian version of the Christian faith in Scotland and in Anglicanism in England, also tempts the dominant groups to some unofficial forms of pretension which are absent in America.

Religious toleration through religiously inspired humility and charity is always a difficult achievement. It requires that religious convictions be sincerely and devoutly held while yet the sinful and finite corruptions of these convictions be humbly acknowledged; and the actual fruits of other faiths be generously estimated. Whenever the religious groups of a community are incapable of such humility and charity the national community will be forced to save its unity through either secularism or authoritarianism.

III

Modern nations have become increasingly heterogeneous ethnically despite the fact that all nations do have a core of ethnic homogeneity. Ethnic pluralism is particularly marked in American life because we have been peopled by the nations of Europe. The fact that, in the wide expanse of American life, racial self-consciousness tended to disintegrate and that the American "melting-pot" actually reduced ethnic groups, which remained in conflict in Europe, to a common amalgam, has accentuated the characteristic universalistic illusions of liberal "children of light." We have regarded racial prejudices as vestiges of barbarism, which an enlightened education was in the process of overcoming. We were certain, in any event, that racial amalgamation would take place in our nation and were inclined to draw from this fact the most ambitious universalistic conclusions; we thought modern history might be a process of a global assimilation of the races. Our anthropologists rightly insisted that there were no biological roots of inequality between races; and they wrongly drew the conclusion from this fact that racial prejudice is a form of ignorance which could be progressively dispelled by enlightenment.

Racial prejudice is indeed a form of irrationality; but it is not as capricious as modern universalists assume. Racial prejudice, the contempt of the other group, is an inevitable concomitant of racial pride; and racial pride is an inevitable concomitant of the ethnic will to live. Wherever life becomes collectively integrated it generates a collective, as well as an individual, survival impulse. But, as previously observed in dealing with individual life, human life is never content with mere physical survival. There are spiritual elements in every human survival impulse; and the corruption of these elements is pride and the will-to-power. This corruption is deeper and more universal than is understood in our liberal culture. Recently an astute war correspondent, in reporting on the life of American soldiers in Africa, spoke of the amazement of the average American soldier over the inability of the natives to understand English and his anger when they refused to understand even when he spoke louder. The natural inclination to regard a foreign language as gibberish and to en-

force understanding of our own language by rais-
ing our voices is a pathetic and true expression of
man's incapacity to comprehend his own finiteness
and to achieve full consciousness of the particular
and unique quality of his own modes of life. This
is the root of his pride; of his tendency to make his
own standards the final norms of existence and to
judge others for failure to conform to them.

This irrationality presents a perpetual hazard
to group relations and makes frictions between
groups an inevitable concomitant of group existence. Even while American liberalism anticipated
a frictionless harmony of ethnic groups and their
eventual assimilation in one racial unity, public
pressure prompted legislation which gave prefer-
ence to north-European groups in our policy of
immigration, thereby proving that our real convictions, in distinction from our pretensions, were that
the American amalgam should not contain too high
a proportion of Latin or Slav ingredients.

In even more serious conflict with our avowed
pretensions is our attitude toward the Negroes.
The real crime of any minority group is that it
diverges from the dominant type; most of the ac-
cusations levelled at these groups are rationalizations of the prejudice aroused by this divergence.

The particular crime of the Negroes is that they diverge too obviously from type. They are black. They have their own characteristic virtues and weaknesses as all ethnic groups have; but racial prejudice makes it impossible for the majority to give generous recognition of virtues and attainments (the artistic gifts of the Negroes for instance) or to discount the frailties of the minority as either weaknesses which are very similar to those of the dominant group or as being different in kind and not in degree from those of the majority.

The case of the Jews presents an equally difficult problem for modern democratic society. It must be admitted that bourgeois liberalism did emancipate Jewish life from the restraints of the medieval ghetto. By creating an impersonal society in which money and credit relations became more important than organic ties it laid the foundations for ethnic pluralism. But the hope that the liberties derived from this situation would be infinitely extensible has proved to be mistaken. While fascist mania and fury have aggravated Anti-Semitism and while some of the noxious fruits of race prejudice which have recently been harvested in the democratic world must be attributed to seeds scattered by the Nazis, we should be blind to attribute this evil altogether to this one specific cause. The Nazis have accentuated but they did not create racial pride. The ideals of democracy do contradict this pride; but it is an illusion of idealistic children of light to imagine that we can destroy evil merely by avowing ideals. The ideal of racial brotherhood is the "law of God" in which we delight "after the inward man"; but racial arrogance is "the law in our members which wars against the law that is in our mind."

Racial bigots bring all kinds of charges against the Jewish minority; but these charges are rationalizations of a profounder prejudice. The real sin of the Jews is twofold. They are first of all a nation scattered among the nations; and therefore they cannot afford to become completely assimilated within the nations; for that would mean the sacrifice of their ethnic existence. Secondly, they are a group which affronts us by diverging doubly from the dominant type, both ethnically and culturally. It is idle to speculate on whether the primary source of Anti-Semitism is racial or religious; for the power of the prejudice is derived from the double divergence. If the Jews were only a religious and not an ethnic group, as some of them claim to be, they would arouse some prejudice by their cultural uniqueness. If they were only a unique ethnic group with the same religion as the majority they would also arouse prejudice. But in either case the prejudice would be more moderate. They are actually an ethnic group with a universalistic religious faith which transcends the values of a single people but which they are forced to use as an instrument of survival in an alien world.

There is no simple solution for a problem of such complexity. No democratic society can afford to capitulate to the pride of dominant groups. The final end of such appeasement is the primitivistic homogeneity of Nazism. On the other hand it is foolish to regard race pride as a mere vestige of barbarism when it is in fact a perpetual source of conflict in human life.

A democratic society must use every stratagem of education and every resource of religion to generate appreciation of the virtues and good intentions of minority groups, which diverge from the type of the majority, and to prompt humility and charity in the life of the majority. It must seek to establish contacts between the groups and prevent the aggravation of prejudice through segregation. It must uncover the peculiar hazards to right judgment which reveal themselves in inter-group relations. A democratic society must, in other words, seek proximate solutions for this problem in indeterminate creative ventures. But the solutions will be more, rather than less, creative if democratic idealists understand the depth of the problem with which they are dealing.

Without this understanding the humility necessary for the achievement of democratic good-will is lacking. The foolish children of light are always seeking to mitigate race prejudice merely by championing the minority groups and by seeking to prove that they are not as bad as their detractors claim them to be. This procedure preserves the proud illusion of the majority that its "mind" is the final bar of judgment before which all nations and peoples must be brought. It would be more helpful if we began with the truer assumption that there is no unprejudiced mind and nc judgment which is not, at least partially, corrupted by pride. The assumption must include the mind and the judgment of the pure idealists who imagine themselves emancipated of all prejudice but frequently manage to express a covert prejudice in their benevolent condescension.

Upon the basis of such a presupposition we could work indeterminately on many proximate solutions for the problem of ethnic pluralism. Our knowledge that there is no complete solution for the problem would save us from resting in some proximate solution under the illusion that it is an ultimate one.

IV

We have considered some aspects of the class struggle in modern society in our analysis of the conflicting attitudes toward property held by the middle and the industrial classes. The classes of modern industrial society are more complex and dynamic than those of the older agrarian order. The interests of various classes are not as completely contradictory to each other as is assumed in Marxism, nor can the classes be as easily reduced to two opposing classes as Marxism believes. The agrarian groups in an industrial society are neither capitalists nor proletarians; and it is both idle and dangerous to force them to choose between these two class positions. The middle class is moreover endlessly proliferated. A small group at the top is undoubtedly primarily governed in its political and economic attitudes by its possession of economic power. There is also a group of managers who wield power through the expertness of their manipulation of economic process without possessing any great power of ownership. There is furthermore a professional class which has a position of relative detachment from the ideological struggles between owners and workers. And finally there is a lower middle class of small tradesmen and clerks, which is much larger and much more stubborn in maintaining itself than Marxism thought possible. It is on the whole a politically incompetent class; yet fascist demagogues have been able to weld the fears and resentments of this class into a positive and demonic political force.

Furthermore the classes of industrial workers easily become divided into the skilled and the unskilled or the employed and the unemployed. In America the former division has produced the schism between the American Federation of Labor and the Congress of Industrial Organization, the former of which expresses conservative political attitudes, including a touching devotion to "free enterprise," which gives its pronouncements a tone, strikingly similar to the statements of the National Association of Manufacturers.

Yet the Marxist picture of a class struggle between the propertied and the propertyless is partly true to the realities; for the most dynamic and sharply defined class forces are those whose attitudes are determined by the possession or lack of property. But the picture is also partly false; for it does not do justice to the endless complexity and the comparative fluidity of the class structure in a democracy.

The multifarious character of the class structure in modern industrial communities is a very considerable resource for the continued health of the democratic state. The various classes which hold a mediating position between the two extremes prevent the class conflict from assuming absolutely critical proportions. Thus the healthier modern democracies have used the political power, derived from the right of suffrage held by the poor, to circumscribe the economic power of the propertied classes. On the other hand the complexity of the class structure may also produce a confusion of forces which may immobilize the government which finds itself at the center of a vortex of class forces, no group having sufficient power to move in a positive direction and all of them having enough power to prevent positive action. This was, in a sense, the situation which destroyed parliamentary government in Germany.

Democracy may thus be destroyed by a confusion of class forces as well as by a civil war in which the extreme classes are pitted against each other and draw the mediating classes into their orbits. The ideal possibility is that the debate between classes should issue, not in an impasse which makes progressive justice impossible, but that it should gradually shift the political institutions of the community to conform to changing economic needs and unchanging demands for a higher justice.

It is not at all certain that any modern democracy, not yet destroyed by class conflict, as Germany and France were destroyed, will be able to achieve the two prerequisites for growth and development within terms of freedom. The one requirement is that there be some equilibrium between class forces; and the other is that the equilibrium should not become static but be subject to the shifts of power which conform to the development of the economic and social situation.

These two requirements can be fulfilled only if the proponents of various political theories have some decent and humble recognition of the fact that their theories are always partly the rationalization of their interests. A conservative class which makes "free enterprise" the final good of the community, and a radical class which mistakes some proximate solution of the economic problem for the ultimate solution of every issue of life, are equally perilous to the peace of the community and to the preservation of democracy. It is a tragic fact that the civil war which threatens democratic communities, has been created by two schools of foolish children of light, each of which failed to recognize the corruption of particular interest in ostensibly universal social ideals. Bourgeois liberalism was on the whole completely unconscious of the corruption of its own class interest and fondly imagined its perspectives to be ultimate. Marxism understood the class corruption in bourgeois perspectives; but its theory of ideology was not profound enough to reveal the fact that the industrial worker had his own peculiar and unique approach to the social issues, which would not appeal to other groups (the agrarian for instance) as final and true. This error lies at the basis of the Marxist fanaticism and absolutism and imperils the democratic process.

The debate between those who see the necessity of freedom and those who desire more social control in the community is not a merely ideological conflict and the opposing protagonists are not merely rationalizing their class interests. The issue

is a real one; and that means that the two positions are not equally false or equally true. Since
freedom and community are partially contradictory and partially complementary values in human
life, there is, however, no perfect solution for the
relation of the two values to each other. This means
that the debate on how much or how little the economic process should be brought under political
control is a never-ending one.

On the other hand there is always an "ideological" element in the debate. Those who have
great power and would like to preserve it, desire
a social situation in which "individual initiative"
will be preserved. Those on the other hand who
are particularly exposed to the perils of a highly
interdependent industrial process and who period-
ically become victims of its dislocations and mal-
adjustments, naturally desire "social security" as
the primary goal of the community.

It is interesting to observe that the preservation
of democratic mutuality between class groups finally depends upon the same quality of religious
humility which is a prerequisite of ethnic and cultural pluralism in a democracy. Religious idealists
usually insist that the primary contribution of religion to democratic life is the cultivation of a

moral idealism which inculcates concern for the other rather than the self. But this is only part of the contribution which a profound religion can make. Consistent egotists would, of course, wreck any democratic process; for it requires some decent consideration of the needs of others. But some of the greatest perils to democracy arise from the fanaticism of moral idealists who are not conscious of the corruption of self-interest in their professed ideals. Democracy therefore requires something more than a religious devotion to moral ideals. It requires religious humility. Every absolute devotion to relative political ends (and all political ends are relative) is a threat to communal peace. But religious humility is no simple moral or political achievement. It springs only from the depth of a religion which confronts the individual with a more ultimate majesty and purity than all human majesties and values, and persuades him to confess: "Why callest thou me good? there is none good but one, that is, God."

The real point of contact between democracy and profound religion is in the spirit of humility which democracy requires and which must be one of the fruits of religion. Democratic life requires a spirit of tolerant cooperation between individuals and groups which can be achieved by neither moral cynics, who know no law beyond their own interest, nor by moral idealists, who acknowledge such a law but are unconscious of the corruption which insinuates itself into the statement of it by even the most disinterested idealists. Democracy may be challenged from without by the force of barbarism and the creed of cynicism. But its internal peril lies in the conflict of various schools and classes of idealists, who profess different ideals but exhibit a common conviction that their own ideals are perfect.

CHAPTER FIVE

THE WORLD COMMUNITY

I

THE ORGANIZATION OF, and the achievement of peace and justice in, the community have been considered up to this point with the understanding that the national community was usually under consideration, but that the social problem of mankind transcended the national community, though the nation has been for some centuries the only effective organ of social cohesion and cooperation. Beyond the national (and in a few cases the imperial) community lies international chaos, slightly qualified by minimal forms of international cooperation.

The problem of overcoming this chaos and of extending the principle of community to worldwide terms has become the most urgent of all the issues which face our epoch. The crisis of our age is undoubtedly due primarily to the fact that the

requirements of a technical civilization have out-
run the limited order which national communities
have achieved, while the resources of our civilization have not been adequate for the creation of
political instruments of order, wide enough to meet
these requirements.

The special urgency under which we stand in
dealing with the problem of the world community
has been occasioned by the convergence of two
forces of universality, one very old and one very
new. For the first time in human history the communal order, which rests upon, and is limited by,
forces of national particularity, stands under a
double challenge. The old force of universality which
challenges nationalistic particularism is the sense
of universal moral obligation, transcending the geographic and other limits of historic communities.
The new force of universality is the global interdependence of nations, ·achieved by a technical
civilization.

The older form of moral universalism is the fruit
of high religions and philosophies which supplanted
tribal and imperial religions some two to three
thousand years ago. Primitive society felt no strong
sense of obligation to life outside of the tribal community, which was held together and limited by

the principle of consanguinity. The early empires were achievements of human freedom over the limits of nature in the sense that they extended the boundaries of effective community beyond the limited force of consanguinity. They were artifacts of the human imagination in which the soldier's skill and the priest's manipulation of religious loyalties achieved a wider community than merely natural impulses could have held together. But these imperial communities were informed by a culture which culminated in an imperial religion, unable to envisage a universal history or to comprehend the totality of human existence in its universe of meaning.

The first religious apprehension of a universal and unlimited moral obligation was achieved in prophetic monotheism, which had its inception in the prophet Amos' conception of a universal history, over which the God of Israel presided as sovereign but of which the history of Israel was not the center and end. Amos thought of the "Holy One of Israel" as a transcendent God who would both use and reject the special mission of Israel in his universal designs and who could taunt his own people with the words, "Are ye not as children of the Ethiopians unto me?" The religion of

Persia culminated in a Zoroastrian universalism, possibly at an earlier, but probably at a later, date. Hebraic prophetism gave rise to an apocalyptic movement in which nationalistic and universalistic motifs were at war with each other; and Christian universalism was born in the atmosphere of this apocalyptic movement, proclaiming to the world that, "In Christ there is neither Jew nor Greek." In western culture Stoic universalism was added to, and became absorbed in, a universal religion which had its first rise in prophetic monotheism. Even Platonic and Aristotelian philosophy, though strongly infected with Greek parochialism, contained universalistic overtones, which made their contribution to the new universalism of western culture.

In China the very slight universalistic overtones in the thought of Confucius were extended by Mencius and others; and were transcended in Laotze's mystic universalism. In India the nationally bound religion of Hinduism was the soil out of which the universally valid Buddhistic scheme of salvation sprang. While the religions of the east were generally too mystic and otherworldly to give historic potency to universal ideals, their emerging universal perspectives must be counted as added evi-

dence of the fact that there has been a general
development in human culture toward the culmination of religions and philosophies in which the
meaning of life and its obligations were interpreted
above and beyond the limits of any particular community.

In the more than two millennia between the rise
of universalistic philosophies and religions and the
present day, nations and empires have risen and
fallen, and national and imperial cultures have
competed, and been compounded, with one another in great profusion. But it seemed a fixed principle of history that the effective human community should be much smaller than the universal
community which was implied in any rigorous analysis of man's obligation to his fellowmen. In this
whole long period of history the national and imperial communities, which gave effective social cohesion to human life, drew a considerable part of
their force of cohesion from the power of particularity. Geographic boundary, ethnic homogeneity
and some common experience and tradition were
the primary bases of their unity.

This state of affairs lasted so long that it seemed
to be an immutable fact of history. It seemed to
prove that men might achieve sufficient freedom

from natural limitations to envisage a universal community, but not sufficient freedom to create it. There seemed no final limit to the size which communities might achieve, except the one limit that they could not embody the entire community of mankind.

So matters stood until a technical civilization, developed during the past century, introduced a new force of universality into history. Its instruments of production, transport and communication reduced the space-time dimensions of the world to a fraction of their previous size and led to a phenomenal increase in the interdependence of all national communities. This new technical interdependence created a potential world community because it established complex interrelations which could be ordered only by a wider community than now exists.

A technical civilization added a natural force of universality to the previously existing moral force. Technical instruments for the conquest of space and time are not natural forces in the same sense as are the limits of geography which they have overcome. They are in fact high achievements of man's ingenuity. But they belong to a quasi-natural realm, not only because they are primarily extensions of man's physical capacities but also because they were not consciously intended to create the universal interdependence which they have in fact achieved. They did increase the power of human hands, feet, eyes and ears to such a degree that all historical processes were given a new dimension. But the moral and social situation which develops from the extension of technics is a by-product and not the conscious end of these inventions.

The development of technics thus confronted our epoch with a new situation. The political institutions of national particularity were no longer challenged merely from above but also from below. From above they felt the impact of the sense of universal moral obligation and from below they were under pressure from the new technical-natural fact of a global economy.

The convergence of two forces of universality, one moral and the other technical, creates such a powerful impetus toward the establishment of a world community that the children of light regard it as a practically inevitable achievement. As always, they underestimate the power of particular forces in history. It is significant that a potential world community announces itself to history by the extension of conflict between nations to global proportions. Two world wars in one generation prove that the logic of history has less power over the recalcitrance of human wills than the children of light assume.

The pride of nations is not easily brought under the dominion of the universal principle, even when the latter is doubly armed. One reason why this is so is that some of the armament of universality is appropriated by egoistic forces in history. The same technical situation which makes a universal community ultimately imperative, also arms particular nations, empires and centers of power with the instruments which make the unification of the world through imperialistic domination seem plausible, if not actually possible. The Nazi effort to unify the world under the dominion of a master race came close enough to success to prove how easily universal forces in history may be appropriated and corrupted for egoistic ends. Long before a genuine universal community can be established mankind must go through a period in which corrupt forms of universalism must be defeated.

The battle for a stable world order is not even won when dynamic forms of imperialism are finally defeated. We shall find in the next decades, and perhaps centuries, that the pride of the great victorious powers will present a less dynamic, but yet a potent, peril to the achievement of world community. The great civilized nations are sufficiently children of light to refrain from efforts at the tyrannical unification of the world. But each of the great powers has sufficient strength to be tempted by the hope that it may establish its own security without too much concern for the security of others and without binding commitments to the common interests of all nations.

This negative form of national egotism, most simply defined as isolationism, will remain a temptation for the great powers for some time to come, however incompatible it may be with the ultimate necessities of the world community. It has at least one element in common with the more dynamic and demonic form of imperialism which mankind has overcome at great cost. It also represents a compound of universalistic and egoistic elements in history; for the great nations which have achieved the strength to indulge in the illusory hope of security by their own power, have their strength by reason of a process of centralization of power in a technical society. Technical processes have accentuated the principle that "to him who hath, shall be given." It operates in international relations, no less than in the economic life of nations.

The fact that the instruments of universality can be temporarily borrowed by the forces of particularity makes the final struggle between particular and universal forces in history a much more tragic chapter of history than the children of light are able to realize. We may live for quite a long time in a period of history in which a potential world community, failing to become actual, will give rise to global, rather than limited, conditions of international anarchy and in which the technics of civilization will be used to aggravate the fury of conflict.

II

During the whole past century, and more particularly since the First World War, our liberal children of light have spawned innumerable plans for world order, all of which were characterized by the typical illusions of simple universalists. They were all based upon the assumption that the logic which inheres in the universal character of the moral imperative and in the global interdependence of a technical civilization would naturally and inevitably bring the political institutions of mankind into conformity with it. They all underesti-

mated the power of particular and limited vitalities in human history. They failed to understand
the persistence and power of the pride of nations
or to comprehend the inertial force of traditional
loyalties.

The children of light in our era might be divided into two schools, one more naïve and the
other a little more sophisticated. The more naïve
school of universalists believes that it would be
sufficient to embody a moral imperative into a universally accepted law. They conceive human history, not as a vast realm of vitalities in which ideas
and ideals are the instruments of conflict as well as
tools for composing it; but rather as a realm of
ideas in which ultimate ideals are bound to bring
warring vitalities under their dominion. They imagine that nations insist upon absolute sovereignty
only because we have had a "natural law" which
justified such sovereignty; and that therefore a new
definition of international law, which denied the
principle of the absolute sovereignty of nations,
would serve to annul the fact.[1] They think that
we lack an international government only because
no one has conceived a proper blueprint of it.

---

[1] A characteristic expression of this faith may be found in
Gerhart Niemeyer's *Law Without Force.*

Therefore they produce such blueprints in great profusion. These pure constitutionalists have a touching faith in the power of a formula over the raw stuff of human history.

The school of more naïve idealists, however, is not sufficiently numerous to warrant much attention. Far more numerous is a school of more sophisticated idealists who recognize that power is required in the organization of all human communities. They would therefore create an international authority, associate an international court with the authority, and provide it with an international police force so that it would have power to enforce its decisions. With these constitutional instruments they would be ready to overcome international anarchy and solve all problems of the world community of nations. These idealists know that force must provide sanctions for law; but they do not understand the complex and various elements which compose the authority for which force is an instrument and only an instrument. They also have a too neat view of the organic processes of history by which communities coalesce and communal authorities are established. They estimate the problem of building communities in purely constitutional terms because they do not recognize or understand the vital social processes which underlie constitutional forms and of which these forms are only instruments and symbols.[2]

While a single sovereignty may be the final and indispensable instrument of a common community, it is not possible to achieve unity by the power of government alone. Government may be the head of the body, which without a single head could not be, or become, a single body; but it is not possible for a head to create a body. The communities of the world, imperial and national, which have achieved a high degree of integration, all have had some core of ethnic homogeneity, though various and heterogeneous elements may be on the periphery. They have also been bound together by particular and unique cultural forces and by the power of a common tradition and of common experiences. The authority of the government in such communities is not infrequently derived from the same history from which the community derived its unity. The prestige of the House of Orange in Holland, for instance, is intimately related to the history of the Dutch emancipation from Spain. Not

---

[2]Mortimer J. Adler's *How To Think About War and Peace* is typical of the school of thought which regards government as the primary, and almost the sole, basis of the unity of the community.

infrequently the source of unity in a national community, the root of its collective self-consciousness, is provided by the experience of facing a common foe. This experience of arriving at communal self-consciousness through encounter with an enemy is a particularly significant symbol of the rôle which particularity plays in establishing national communities. Geographic limitation, ethnic and cultural uniqueness distinguishing this from other communities, and a common history, usually embodying comradeship in meeting a common foe, all contribute to the cohesion of communities. Governments develop to express and to perfect the unity thus achieved, but they do not create what they must presuppose.

America has produced so many pure constitutionalists in international political theory partly because American history encourages the illusion that the nation was created purely by constitutional fiat and compact. This is an illusion because the constitution was the end and not the beginning of an historical process which began with a common conflict against an imperial overlord. In this conflict the separate colonial entities gradually coalesced into a single community. In its course a military leader emerged, in the person of Washington, whose

prestige was of immeasurable importance as a rally-
ing point for a united nation. Most modern nations
do not have as clear a constitutional beginning as
the United States. It is therefore the more significant that even in the history of the United States
the real beginning is more organic and less constitutional than is usually assumed.

It cannot be denied that modern nations and
empires have been able to extend their dominion
and to include within their original community
many and various other communities which do not
have obvious affinities with the original basis of
unity. This policy is not always successful. In the
case of Great Britain, Scotland and Wales could
be amalgamated into a wider unity but Ireland
could not. But even when it is successful, idealists
are wrong in assuming that this process is infinitely
extensible until the government of the world is
finally achieved. They do not see that the power
of some particular, limited and unique historical
vitality and experience creates the original core of
community and the original prestige and authority
of its government; and that even in its most complex elaborations an advanced community contin-
ues to depend partly upon this power for its cohesion and for the authority of its government.

This is why the transition from a particular to a universal community is a more difficult step than is usually assumed. It is a step different not merely in degree from those which have marked the development of larger and larger communities in the history of mankind. It is different in kind. It is in fact so completely different that we cannot be certain that it is a step within the possibilities of history. If it is within the possibilities, only desperate necessity makes it so. Yet we may be sure that ages of tragic history will be required to achieve what is so impossible and yet so necessary.

It may be regarded as axiomatic that the less a community is held together by cohesive forces in the texture of its life the more must it be held together by power. This fact leads to the dismal conclusion that the international community lacking these inner cohesive forces, must find its first unity through coercive force to a larger degree than is compatible with the necessities of justice. Order will have to be purchased at the price of justice; though it is quite obvious that if too much justice is sacrificed to the necessities of order, the order will prove too vexatious to last. For a long time to come the international community will have few elements of inner cohesion, or benefit from the

unity of a common culture or tradition. It will possess only two minimal forces of cohesion: a common overtone of universality in its moral ideals,
and the fear of anarchy. The fear of anarchy will
undoubtedly be the more potent of these two; but
this fear is certainly not as powerful as the fear of
a common and concrete foe.

However, it may be idle to estimate the perils
of world unity through preponderant power when
we face another and previous issue, which the
purer constitutionalists have not fully considered.
Most plans for a constitutional world order, presented by the children of light, assume that it
would be a fairly easy achievement for nations to
abridge their sovereignty in favour of a new international authority. They think in terms of a possible world constitutional convention which would
set up the authority and would then call upon the
nations to subordinate their interests to this new
sovereignty. This hope is a projection of the "social
contract" theory of government, characteristic of
bourgeois thought, to the scale of the world community. We have previously considered the error
of excessive voluntarism which underlies this theory. This voluntarism attributes too much power
to the human will, particularly to the collective will

of men. It fails to understand the pertinence of the
Pauline confession: "For to will is present with
me; but how to perform that which is good I find
not."[3]

The history of the past decade is a sad but ir-
refutable proof of the truth of this confession, particularly as applied to the motives and actions of
nations. For all civilized nations had a stronger
desire to come to the aid of stricken peoples than
they had power to act upon that desire. This "defect of the will" stands between the conviction of
nations that they ought to abridge their sovereignty
and their capacity to do what they ought by a clear
act of renunciation. Every impulse of national
pride intervenes to prevent the desired, or at least
desirable, action.[4]

The inability of nations to renounce their power

---

[3]Romans 7:18.

[4]A recent contretemps in international relations offers an
interesting sidelight on the ethics of nations. A British minister,
Oliver Lyttleton, wishing to pay us a compliment, declared
that the Japanese attack did not force us into the war because
we had really provoked the attack by our unneutral interest
in the cause of the victims of aggression. This compliment was
widely resented in America because it challenged the official
interpretation, that we were involved in the war because we
were attacked and our own interests were imperiled. A modern
nation does not dare to go to war for reasons other than those
of self-interest and cannot conduct the war without claiming
to be motivated by higher motives than those of self-interest.
The British minister had failed to do justice to these subtleties.

or qualify their freedom by explicit act means that
the processes of history toward unity are more tor-
tuous than is envisaged in pure constitutional theory. At the present moment the smaller nations
are being subjected to the abridgement of sovereignty by the forces of history which centralize effective power in the hands of the great nations. But
this development accentuates, rather than weakens,
the power of the great nations. The international
politics of the coming decades will be dominated
by great powers who will be able to prevent recalcitrance among the smaller nations, but who will
have difficulty in keeping peace between each other
because they will not have any authority above
their own powerful enough to bend or deflect their
wills. Furthermore they will be powerful enough
to create systems of unilateral security, which will
not be adequate for the preservation of peace, but
will seem adequate for their own protection.

Whatever unity may be achieved in the coming
decades must be attained by the coalescence of
power and the development of a core of international community among the great powers. In
so far as their common efforts in a world struggle
have led to the implicit abridgement of sovereignty,
a world alliance, which wins a global war may be

regarded as the potential center of a world community. But it is not certain that this potential center will be actualized after the war is over. The abridgements of sovereignty implicit in the mutual accords, achieved under the necessities of war and for the purpose of defeating a common foe, are not lasting, in so far as the fear of the common foe has been the primary motive of the mutual accord. No doubt there is a general appreciation among the great powers of the peril of international anarchy; and this appreciation may serve to preserve war-time accords. But since the fear of anarchy is less potent than the fear of a concrete foe, the general tendency will be for war-time accords to be weakened rather than strengthened. The possibility of a merger of sovereignties between the great powers into a single center of authority must certainly be regarded as very remote. When it is remembered that many modern and ancient nations (including England and Russia) achieved national unity only because a foreign conqueror superimposed the initial core of unity, it will be seen that a more historical and organic development toward world unity is almost as difficult as a purely constitutional one. For there is not one center of power and community in the world, great and good enough to superimpose the first pattern of unity upon the diverse and competing national forces. There are three or four great centers, which will not find it easy to reach a strong accord with each other. If they should fail, their failure would result in further world conflict in which the units of conflict would be even greater and more sharply defined.

III

All these difficulties are sufficiently apparent to prompt the emergence of realistical as well as idealistic interpretations of the global task which faces our age. While America has produced more idealistic plans for world order than realistic ones, the realistic approach has also been attempted in both Britain and America. It is indicative of the spiritual problem of mankind that these realistic approaches are often as close to the abyss of cynicism as the idealistic approaches are to the fog of sentimentality.

The realistic school of international thought believes that world politics cannot rise higher than the balance-of-power principle. The balance-of-power theory of world politics,[5] seeing no possibility of a genuine unity of the nations, seeks to construct the most adequate possible mechanism for equilibrating power on a world scale. Such a policy, which holds all factors in the world situation in the most perfect possible equipoise, can undoubtedly mitigate anarchy. A balance of power is in fact a kind of managed anarchy. But it is a system in which anarchy invariably overcomes the management in the end. Despite its defects the policy of the balance of power is not as iniquitous as idealists would have us believe. For even the most perfectly organized society must seek for a decent equilibrium of the vitalities and forces under its organization. If this is not done, strong disproportions of power develop; and wherever power is inordinate, injustice results. But an equilibrium of power without the organizing and equilibrating force of government, is potential anarchy which becomes actual anarchy in the long run.

The balance-of-power system may, despite its

---

[5]Nicholas Spykman's *America's Strategy in World Politics* is the ablest exposition of the balance-of-power policy in international relations. Spykman believes that America, rather than Britain, must manage the balance in the future, partly because the world, rather than Europe, has become the realm in which the significant forces, which must be balanced, express themselves.

defects, become the actual consequence of present policies. The peace of the world may be maintained perilously and tentatively, for some decades, by an uneasy equilibrium between the three great powers, America, Russia and Britain. Field Marshal Smuts' suggestion that Britain must strengthen its position by the inclusion of friendly continental nations into the British Commonwealth of Nations, presupposes such a development and naturally seeks to strengthen the British position so that it will be more equally balanced with the potentially more powerful American and Russian allies.

While a balance between the great powers may be the actual consequence of present policies, it is quite easy to foreshadow the doom of such a system. No participant in a balance is ever quite satisfied with its own position. Every center of power will seek to improve its position: and every such effort will be regarded by the others as an attempt to disturb the equilibrium. There is sufficient mistrust between the great nations, even while they are still locked in the intimate embrace of a great common effort, to make it quite certain that a mere equilibrium between them will not suffice to preserve the peace.

Thus a purely realistic approach to the problem of world community offers as little hope of escape from anarchy as a purely idealistic one. Clearly it has become necessary for the children of light to borrow some of the wisdom of the children of darkness; and yet be careful not to borrow too much. Pure idealists underestimate the 'perennial power of particular and parochial loyalties, operating as a counter force against the achievement of a wider community. But the realists are usually so impressed by the power of these perennial forces that they fail to recognize the novel and unique elements in a revolutionary world situation. The idealists erroneously imagine that a new situation automatically generates the resources for the solution of its problem. The realists erroneously discount the destructive, as well as the creative, power of a revolutionary situation. A catastrophic period of history may not create all the resources required for the solution of its problems; but it does finally destroy some false solutions and some of the inertial obstacles to advance. A view more sober than that of either idealists or realists must persuade us that,

"If hopes are dupes,
Fears may be liars."

IV

A sober approach to the world situation must begin with the assumption that the initial basis of unity for the world must be laid in a stable accord between the great powers. It may not be possible to achieve such an accord. Even if achieved it will probably be qualified by regional arrangements. A policy of unilateral security for each great power may be artfully compounded with a wider system of mutual security. We shall probably not know for some years to come whether an agreement between the great powers represents a genuine system of mutual security or whether it is merely a façade for a policy of partitioning the world into spheres of influence. Subsequent events, rather than present policies, may determine the final outcome.

It is at any rate quite clear that only the preponderant power of the great nations can be an adequate core of authority for a minimal world order. The vitalities of the world community are too diverse, the cultural and ethnic forces too heterogeneous and the elements of common tradition and experience too minimal to allow us to dispense with the policy of establishing preponderant collective power as the initial basis of world order.

A mere alliance of great nations would of course degenerate into an insufferable imperialism. A political realism which advocated such a policy, without immediately considering what kind of checks could be placed upon the central core of power, would represent a too complete appropriation of the wisdom of the children of darkness; and would result in works of darkness. The actual situation is that the first task of a community is to subdue chaos and create order; but the second task is equally important and must be implicated in the first. That task is to prevent the power, by which initial unity is achieved, from becoming tyrannical.

Justice is introduced into a field of order if the organizing power is placed under both moral and constitutional checks. Neither type of restraint is easily placed upon the inchoate world government of an alliance of great powers. Yet both are not completely outside the realm of historical possibility.

The possibility of placing constitutional checks upon the power of the great nations, who must furnish the core of the world community, lies in the fact that they will find it impossible to reach a stable accord with each other if they do not embody plans for the organization of the world into their agreements. The continents, particularly Europe and Asia, lie between them. The sovereignties of these continents are mutilated and the economic life is in chaos. Continued chaos in these continents would sow discord between the great nations; for it would tempt each great power to attempt the extension of its influence. Only mutual agreement will make a broad restoration possible. But such agreements must draw the smaller powers into the instruments of agreement. The world which lies between the great powers is too complex to make a simple partnership between them possible. Only careful plans, reaching beyond the immediate interests of the great nations, and inevitably drawing the smaller nations into the partnership, will suffice. But such plans will inevitably arm the smaller powers with constitutional instruments for the protection of their rights and the assertion of such power as they possess. Thus constitutional principles will inevitably be brought into the more organic processes of history and become integral to them.

We cannot assume that considerations of justice alone would persuade the great powers to allow constitutional restraints upon their authority to develop. Nations, particularly great nations, are usually too proud to understand that their power might be a peril to other nations. The real hope for the development of a system of at least quasi-constitutional restraints upon the power of the great nations lies in the fact that they cannot approach the issues between each other without dealing with the whole field of international life in which their power has become preponderant; and they cannot solve these issues without drawing the smaller powers into their agreements.

Chaos in either Europe or Asia would tempt the great powers to ultimate conflict because each power would seek to organize the chaos, partly out of fear that, if it should fail to do so, one of the other powers would increase its prestige by such organization. Even an agreement between the powers to divide the world into spheres of influence, in which each would be left alone to organize the realm most contiguous to it, would only mitigate mutual suspicion and only slightly delay ultimate conflict; for no delimitation of spheres of influence will cover all areas of the continents or give tolerable health to their economic and political life.

Despite these perils, it is, of course, possible that the great nations will fail to arrive at significant agreements and that their failure will be signalized by the partitioning of the continents. In that case the world would face the peril of anarchy once more rather than the peril of super-imperialism. But the evils of the policy of partitioning the world are so obvious, that we have some right to hope that a rigorous effort will be made to achieve a more basic and lasting accord. The best hope of justice lies in the fact that a stable order is not possible without introducing instruments of justice into the agreements which are to provide for order.

The experience of Abraham Lincoln in dealing with national issues might well instruct us on the relative importance of order and justice in international politics. Facing civil conflict within the nation Lincoln declared: "My primary purpose is to save the union." Analogously our primary purpose must be to create a union. It was significant, however, that though Lincoln was prepared to save the union "half slave and half free" it soon became apparent that this could not be done. The union could be saved only by abolishing slavery. This is a nice symbol of the fact that order precedes justice in the strategy of government; but that only an order which implicates justice can achieve a stable peace. An unjust order quickly invites the resentment and rebellion which lead to its undoing.

V

While political strategies deal with outer and social checks upon the egoism of men and of nations and while no individual or collective expression of human vitality is ever moral enough to obviate the necessity of such checks, it is also true that outer checks are insufficient if some inner moral checks upon human ambition are not effective. Consistently egoistic individuals would require a tyrannical government for the preservation of social order. Fortunately individuals are not consistently egoistic. Therefore democratic government, rather than Thomas Hobbes' absolutism, has proved a possibility in national life. Nations are more consistently egoistic than individuals; yet even the collective behaviour of men stands under some inner moral checks; and the peace of the world requires that these checks be strengthened.

Since no constitutional checks, which may be placed upon the power of the great hegemonic nations, will be fully adequate, it is particularly important that the strongest possible moral restraints be placed upon their power.

Since China is only potentially, and not yet actually, one of these great powers, the peace of the world will depend particularly upon the policies of the three other great powers, Britain, Russia and America. Of these three Russia will have the greatest difficulty in establishing inner moral checks upon its will-to-power. This will be the case not because it is communistic or materialistic; but rather because it is informed by a simple religion and culture which makes self-criticism difficult and self-righteousness inevitable. Its creed assumes the evil intentions of capitalistic powers and the innocency and virtue of a nation which stands on the other side of the revolution. The naïve self-righteousness which flows from these presuppositions is more dangerous to a mutual accord between the nations than any of the real or fancied vices which are attributed to Russia. The tendency toward self-righteousness is accentuated in Russia by the absence of democratic institutions through which, in other nations, sensitive minorities may act as the conscience of the nation and subject its actions and pretensions to criticism.

The so-called democratic and "Christian" nations have a culture which demands self-criticism in principle; and institutions which make it possible in practice. We must not assume, however, that

any modern nation can easily achieve the high virtue of humility; or establish moral checks upon its
power lusts. Britain has certain advantages over
America in this realm for two reasons. The national
interest of Britain is more completely identical with
the interests of the nations than is the case with
the United States; because Britain is more desperately in need of world security for its survival than
America. Secondly, Britain has had longer experience in wielding power in world affairs than America. Through this experience Britain has learned
to exercise critical restraint upon its power impulses to a larger degree than its critics realize.
The critics have fastened upon the inevitable note
of self-righteousness which creeps into the engagement between morals and politics in any national
community. The empire is not so purely an expression of the sense of moral responsibility as the more
uncritical British defenders of empire would have
it appear; but neither is it as simply the expression
of the impulse of domination as the critics of British imperialism believe. Hypocrisy and pretension
are the inevitable concomitants of the engagement
between morals and politics. But they do not arise
where no effort is made to bring the power impulse
of politics under the control of conscience. The

pretension that it has been brought completely under control is thus the hypocritical by-product of the moral endeavour.

Crude American criticisms of British politics are themselves a revelation of our own moral problem. America is potentially more powerful than Britain; but it has had little moral consciousness of its own power. As a result it alternates between moods of complete irresponsibility and of cynicism. In the one mood it would disavow the responsibilities of power because it fears its corruptions. In the other mood it displays an adolescent pride of power and a cynical disregard of its responsibilities.

These moods are marks of a lack of political and moral maturity. They are, in addition to certain constitutional difficulties, the cause of the unpredictable character of American foreign policy. If America achieves maturity, the primary mark of it must be the willingness to assume continuing responsibility in the world community of nations. We must seek to maintain a critical attitude toward our own power impulses; and our self-criticism must be informed by the humble realization of the fact that the possession of great power is a temptation to injustice for any nation. Relative innocency or inexperience in wielding power is no guarantee of virtue. It is on the contrary a hazard to the attainment of virtue. The possession of power on the other hand creates responsibilities which must not be evaded, even though it is known that they cannot be fulfilled without some egoistic corruption.

The field of politics is not helpfully tilled by pure moralists; and the realm of international politics is particularly filled with complexities which do not yield to the approach of a too simple idealism. On the other hand the moral cynicism and defeatism which easily results from a clear-eyed view of the realities of international politics is even more harmful. The world community must be built by men and nations sufficiently mature and robust to understand that political justice is achieved, not merely by destroying, but also by deflecting, beguiling and harnessing residual self-interest and by finding the greatest possible concurrence between self-interest and the general welfare. They must also be humble enough to understand that the forces of self-interest to be deflected are not always those of the opponent or competitor. They are frequently those of the self, individual or collective, including the interests of the idealist who erroneously imagines himself above the battle.

Since all political and moral striving results in

frustration as well as fulfillment, the task of building a world community requires a faith which is not too easily destroyed by frustration. Such a faith must understand the moral ambiguities of history and know them not merely as accidents or as the consequence of the malevolence of this man or that nation; it must understand them as permanent characteristics of man's historic existence. Their manifestation in the field of international relations is more vivid than in any other field; because all aspects of man's historical problems appear upon that larger field in more vivid and discernible proportions.

The task of building a world community is man's final necessity and possibility, but also his final impossibility. It is a necessity and possibility because history is a process which extends the freedom of man over natural process to the point where universality is reached. It is an impossibility because man is, despite his increasing freedom, a finite creature, wedded to time and place and incapable of building any structure of culture or civilization which does not have its foundations in a particular and dated locus.

The world community, standing thus as the final possibility and impossibility of human life, will be in actuality the perpetual problem as well as the constant fulfillment of human hopes.

It will be a long while before modern idealists will recognize that the profundities of the Christian faith, which they have disavowed, are indispensable resources for the historic tasks which lie before us. These profundities were disavowed partly for the good reason that they were corrupted by obscurantism and were intimately related to cultural presuppositions of civilizations, long since destroyed. They were also disavowed for the bad reason that modern culture imagined history itself to be redemptive and therefore was uninterested in profounder interpretations of the relation of history to redemption.

The Christian faith finds the final clue to the meaning of life and history in the Christ whose goodness is at once the virtue which man ought, but does not, achieve in history, and the revelation of a divine mercy which understands and resolves the perpetual contradictions in which history is involved, even on the highest reaches of human achievements. From the standpoint of such a faith it is possible to deal with the ultimate social problem of human history: the creation of community in world dimensions. The insistence of the Christian faith that the love of Christ is the final norm of human existence must express itself socially in unwillingness to stop short of the whole human community in expressing our sense of moral responsibility for the life and welfare of others. The understanding of the Christian faith that the highest achievements of human life are infected with sinful corruption will help men to be prepared for new corruptions on the level of world community which drive simpler idealists to despair. The hope of Christian faith that the divine power which bears history can complete what even the highest human striving must leave incomplete, and can purify the corruptions which appear in even the purest human aspirations, is an indispensable prerequisite for diligent fulfillment of our historic tasks. Without it we are driven to alternate moods of sentimentality and despair; trusting human powers too much in one moment and losing all faith in the meaning of life when we discover the limits of human possibilities.

The world community, toward which all historical forces seem to be driving us, is mankind's final possibility and impossibility. The task of achieving it must be interpreted from the standpoint of a faith which understands the fragmentary and broken character of all historic achievements and yet has confidence in their meaning because it knows their completion to be in the hands of a Divine Power, whose resources are greater than those of men, and whose suffering love can overcome the corruptions of man's achievements, without negating the significance of our striving.